$24.00
592   Petersen, Christine
PET   Invertebrates

SHSLC

Invertebrates

Christine Petersen

Franklin Watts
A Division of Scholastic Inc.
New York Toronto London Auckland Sydney
Mexico City New Delhi Hong Kong
Danbury, Connecticut

For Beth, who makes it
all possible

Photographs © 2002: Aaron Norman: 43; Peter Arnold Inc.: 64, 66 (Fred
Bavendam), 81 (Fred Bruemmer), 107 (Norbert Wu); Photo Researchers, NY: 9
(Biophoto Associates), 10 (Dr. Jeremy Burgess/SPL), 69 (A. Flowers & L. Newman),
104 (Patrick W. Grace), 27, 85 (Andrew J. Martinez), 39 (Fred McConnaughey), 33
left (Neil S. McDaniel), cover (Gregory Ochoki), 92 (Rod Planck), 87 (Mark Smith),
97 (Kenneth H. Thomas), 34 (Stuart Westmorland); Visuals Unlimited: 74 (Bill
Beatty), 20 left (Hal Beral), 54 (R. Calentine), 51 (W.M. Jorgensen), 99 (Bill Kamin),
15 (Ken Lucas), 47 (Science VU), 94 (Rob & Ann Simpson), 82 (Garry Walters), 77
(WHOI), 33 right (David Wrobel).

Library of Congress Cataloging-in-Publication Data

Petersen, Christine.
    Invertebrates / by Christine Petersen
        p. cm.
Includes bibliographical references (p.).
Summary: A close look at past and present invertebrates, including sponges, jellies,
worms, mollusks, and arthropods.

    ISBN 0-531-12021-X
    1. Invertebrates—Juvenile literature. (1. Invertebrates.) 1. Title.
    QL362.4 .P48 2002
    592—dc21
                                            2001003031

Contents

Chapter Seven: Segmented Worms

Chapter Eight: Armored Animals, Part One: Chelicerates, Crustaceans, and Myriapods

Chapter Nine: Armored Animals, Part Two: Insects

Chapter Ten: Echinoderms

CHAPTER ONE

LIFE'S HUMBLE BEGINNINGS

It's almost impossible to comprehend how ancient Earth is. Experts tell us it's about 4,600,000,000 (4.6 billion) years old. And even after all that time, our planet continues to change. Continents move. Climates grow warmer and colder. Ocean levels rise and fall, while mountains bulge up and are worn away.

Earth's current *biodiversity*, or variety of life, is the result of this changing environment. Scientists have already identified more than 1.5 million species living on our planet today. Many, many more—a total of perhaps 5 million to 100 million species—remain to be discovered in Earth's rain forests, deep seas, and other hard-to-reach places. Countless others disappeared long before humans were here to know them.

Only in the past few centuries have people begun to decode Earth's long history and to see how all this diversity came to be.

A BRIEF HISTORY OF EARTH

For much of Earth's early history, there was nothing here that we'd recognize as "home"—no land, no seas, and no life at all.

Our Sun and the nine planets that revolve around it formed roughly five billion years ago from a cloud of dust and gases floating freely in space. Slowly, these particles were pulled inward by gravity and shrank toward the center of the cloud. A dense, fiery ball formed as *atoms* (individual chemical particles) fused together, causing them to radiate heat and light. Dust and gases around this new central mass, the Sun, gathered into their own conglomerates of material and formed nine planets, each with its own spinning orbit.

The young Earth, third planet from the Sun, was probably quite cold at first. Over time, pressure and temperature inside the planet increased. Volcanoes belched hot hydrogen gases into the air and spilled out *lava* (melted rock) that dried like a thin, rocky skin on the planet's surface.

Gases from the volcanoes floated up into space around the planet, forming massive clouds of water vapor. For countless years, rain fell and lightning ripped through the skies. Land masses rose up from Earth's rocky crust, and oceans gathered around them. Finally, the stage was set for the beginnings of life on Earth.

THE INGREDIENTS FOR LIFE

Like a good meal, life requires just the right ingredients to start "cooking." There must be warm sunshine, but not too much heat. Water is essential, too. Oxygen and small amounts of other chemicals, such as carbon and nitrogen, must be available in the planet's atmosphere. Of our Sun's nine circling planets, only Earth has just the right balance of these conditions to support life.

Give some thought to the word *life*. What qualities would you use to separate living and nonliving things? Scientists and philosophers have struggled with this question for centuries. A few common characteristics stand out. To be considered alive, a thing needs a "body"—it must contain at least one *cell*. Next, life requires energy. Cells, therefore, must be able to find and make use of some source of nourishment. Living things usually move and grow as well.

Yet even with all these characteristics to guide us, recognizing life is a challenge. Televisions and rocks aren't living. Mice and trees, by contrast, are clearly alive. But what about crystals like ice and salt? Crystals grow. Fire grows too, and even consumes ("eats") materials to feed itself. Yet neither crystals nor fire can reproduce. Reproduction, then, is another good indicator of true life.

LIFE TAKES HOLD

The earliest signs of life, about 3.5 billion years old, have been found in rocks that are now part of the Australian continent. These

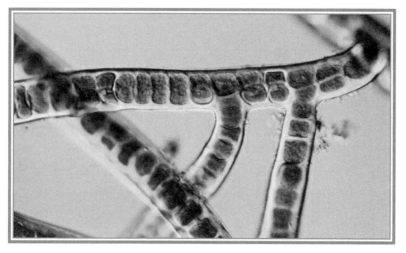

Single-celled cyanobacteria, or blue-green algae, evolved about 3.5 billion years ago and remain the most common form of life on Earth today

first creatures were single cells that used sunlight and the process of *photosynthesis* to convert light into energy. Called *cyanobacteria*, or blue-green algae, these single-celled beings remain the most common forms of life on our planet today.

Earth's early atmosphere contained plenty of *carbon dioxide* (CO_2, a chemical that's poisonous to most life forms today), but very little oxygen. That soon changed. Energy isn't the only product of photosynthesis—oxygen is released as well. For more than a billion years after blue-green algae appeared, oxygen gathered, forming an atmosphere around the planet. Some oxygen atoms formed *ozone*, a molecule (collection of atoms) that hovers in Earth's upper atmosphere and reflects the Sun's burning rays. Protected from the worst of the Sun's heat and from deadly *ultraviolet radiation* by this ozone layer, Earth began to cool. The atmosphere was now filled with oxygen, and Earth's watery environments were ripe for more forms of life to arise.

Under these favorable conditions, single-celled creatures began to diversify. Some learned to eat other cells as food. These are the most ancient ancestors of *animals*. The first multicellular animals were probably groups of single cells that gathered together into *colonies*, each cell becoming specialized for a particular task—feeding, reproducing, and so forth. By about 700 million years ago, multicellular living things were common in the oceans.

Invertebrate animals are those with no backbones. These include sponges, jellyfishes, worms, crabs, octopuses, insects, and many others. Invertebrates evolved very early on and today make up about 95 percent of all species on Earth. *Vertebrate* animals— fish, amphibians, reptiles, birds, and mammals (like you)—have internal skeletons, including backbones, or spines, that support their bodies.

CELLS

For a very long time, no one had any idea that living things are actually made up of many tiny "building blocks" called cells.

In 1665 Robert Hooke, an English scientist, invented a microscope that allowed him to observe objects magnified at thirty times their actual size. Hooke sliced a piece of cork (a kind of tree bark) so thin that it was almost transparent and inspected it under his microscope. What he saw resembled tiny bricks lined up in tidy rows. Hooke called these "little boxes," or cells.

Ten years later, Dutch merchant Antonie van Leeuwenhoek

Robert Hooke's drawing of his own microscope.

invented a much more powerful microscope capable of magnifying objects three hundred times. Van Leeuwenhoek gathered water samples from a nearby pond to observe under the microscope's lens. He couldn't have been more surprised at what he found: tiny creatures swimming through the water. Van Leeuwenhoek was the first person to see living, single-celled creatures.

Although Hooke never realized it, the "little boxes" in his slice of cork were actually the hollowed-out shells of dead plant cells. Animals, in turn, are made of billions of cells similar to the ones discovered in van Leeuwenhoek's pond water. Biologists now recognize that living things are made up of one or more cells and that new cells form from the division of old cells.

MAKING NEW CELLS

Each cell, however small, is like a miniature factory, equipped with all the mechanisms needed to support and reproduce life. The outside layer, or cell membrane, functions something like a gate that controls what moves in and out of the cell. A jellylike substance fills most of the cell's interior and serves as a cushion. Within this jelly are many delicate *organelles* (cell parts), each of which has a specific job to do. Several types of organelles are involved in the collection, transport, breakdown, or storage of food, water, and wastes, regulating the cell's chemical balance. Some organelles build proteins that help the cell grow and repair itself. The *nucleus*, which looks likes a dark blob when seen through a microscope, manages all the cell's functions, builds proteins, and is involved in reproduction. The nucleus contains *DNA (deoxyribonucleic acid)*, the "blueprint" that contains codes for each cell's unique characteristics.

DNA is a large molecule formed by two long chains of smaller *nucleotide* molecules. Four types of nucleotides are found in DNA, linked together and organized into groups called *genes*. Each gene (or sometimes a group of genes) controls a specific characteristic in the organism, such as eye color. Laid out flat, a DNA molecule would look much like a stepladder, with rungs (steps) connecting the pair of strands down their lengths. But DNA isn't flat—the two strands are twisted around each other into a helix, or spiral. The "rungs" are chemical bonds that hold atoms on the two chains together. The nucleus of each cell contains several DNA helixes, each tightly coiled and packaged with proteins to form a *chromosome*. Humans have 46 chromosomes (that's 23 pairs) in the nuclei of their cells, while goldfish have 94 and king crabs have 208.

When it's ready to reproduce, a cell makes a duplicate of its own DNA, using the existing chromosomes as a model. The two DNA copies move to opposite ends of the cell, and the cell membrane pinches down the middle, separating the old cell into two new, identical cells. This is how the early blue-green algae copied themselves. It's a process referred to as *asexual* (without sex) *reproduction*, because DNA from only one individual is involved. In an animal's body, asexual reproduction is used to make new skin cells and blood cells, for example, whenever they're needed.

Within each *species* (a distinct group of organisms that can mate and produce fertile offspring in the wild, without human assistance), the sequence of genes is almost identical. Yet the ways in which those genes express themselves vary from individual to individual, thanks to *sexual reproduction*, or the mixing of DNA that occurs when two individuals mate. This variation accounts for the differences in appearance that we see among the members of our own family—hair color, for example—as well as for traits like right- and left-handedness, blood type, and so on.

When mating, each parent contributes one reproductive cell—a sperm from the male and an egg from the female. These reproductive cells are specially built to contain single chromosomes instead of the chromosome pairs found in regular cells. DNA from the sperm and egg match up and their genes mix. The offspring has a new combination of traits based on the genes inherited from its parents. When offspring go on to reproduce, their offspring will, in turn, have another set of characteristics slightly different from those of their parents and grandparents.

The DNA duplication process usually goes without a hitch. Once in a while, however, a mistake gets made in the "translation" of the DNA blueprint. The result is a slight change, or *mutation*, which can produce a unique trait. Eventually, most mutations turn out to be either harmful or useless to the organism. These usually don't get passed along to the offspring because they reduce the individual's ability to survive and reproduce. Once in a while, however, a mutation turns out to be useful. The new trait provides the individual with some advantage that increases its chance of survival. The mutated gene is then passed down to future generations because the organism is successful enough to reproduce.

Mutations can increase the genetic diversity of a species, but they are not the only force that affects variation. Each time sexual reproduction occurs, the nucleotide "building blocks" in genes are re-sorted to produce slightly different combinations. The success of those new genes is determined by the environment through a process called *natural selection*. Every year, many young animals and plants are born, yet not all live long enough to reproduce. The "survivors" are usually individuals whose combination of traits happens to suit their local climates and food sources. Foxes born with extra-thick fur, for instance, are more likely to survive an especially cold winter than foxes whose hair grows thin and short. In this way, natural selection "chooses" the genes that are passed along. When the environment changes, different traits may be selected.

The Changing Earth

By the early 1800s geologists—scientists who study Earth's formation and history—had learned that Earth's rocky foundations are laid down in layers, like cards in a deck. As they examined layers of rocks in different parts of the world, geologists began to find signs of ancient life, which they called *fossils*. If a plant or animal dies in a place where its body is buried quickly, such as in a swamp or in sand at the bottom of the ocean, its bones may be slowly replaced by minerals, which become part of the surrounding rock. Other signs of ancient life may fossilize, too, if left undisturbed for a long time: footprints, burrows, shells, and teeth are just a few of the items that reveal the presence of creatures that lived long ago.

Some of those earliest fossil discoveries shocked scientists because the fossils looked so different from species we know today. Stranger yet was the fact that groups of fossils changed from one rock layer to the next. Clearly, species have come and gone over the long history of the planet. Modern plants and animals are just the latest in a long line of living things that have made their homes on Earth. Through rocks and their fossil treasures, we find the calendar of life itself: *geologic time*, measured not in minutes, hours, or days, but in millions of years.

The combined effect of these forces—mutation, recombination of genes, and natural selection—and others is known as *evolution*, or the gradual change in species over time.

MAKING SENSE OF NATURAL SELECTION

Throughout the seventeenth and eighteenth centuries, people attempted to explain the diversity of life on Earth. Many believed

Fossils like these ammonites, relatives of octopuses that were common more than 250 million years ago, provide evidence of how life on Earth has changed over time.

that all living things had been created specifically for their roles in the world and therefore would never change. Other scientists suggested that species changed from generation to generation. But until the mid-1800s, no one was able to suggest a method by which such changes might take place.

In 1831 a young Englishman named Charles Darwin sailed with the crew of the H.M.S. *Beagle*, whose five-year mission was to explore and map the continents and islands south of the equator. Darwin spent much of his time collecting specimens of the unfamiliar plants, animals, and fossils he found and observing species in many different environments. He also did a lot of reading, especially about geology and Earth's history. Influenced by the ideas of other scientists, Darwin began to believe that Earth was an extremely ancient place and had undergone many changes over time—including shifts in its diversity of living things. Upon his return to England in 1836, Darwin began to ponder the causes of biological diversity.

Darwin was especially intrigued by a group of finches he had seen on the Galápagos Islands, a chain of thirteen volcanic islands and more than a hundred rocky islets off the western coast of South

America. These finches were not terribly different in appearance from finches he had seen on the South American continent, nor did they look radically different from one another, with one exception: their beaks. Finches are usually seed-eaters with medium-size beaks. When Darwin returned to England and began to study the finches he'd collected from the Galápagos Islands, he noticed a wide range of beak shapes and sizes among them. Some were exceptionally thick, like parrots' beaks. Others looked like swords. Some finches had very tiny, delicate beaks. The shape of a particular finch's beak, it seemed, related to the food it ate. Thick-billed birds could crack hard nut shells. Birds with long bills were able to reach far into holes in trees in search of insects, and birds with small beaks could pick up and eat small seeds.

How could so many different beak shapes and feeding behaviors have come about on a few islands floating in the middle of the ocean? Darwin reasoned that the first finches to inhabit these islands must have lived in South America but were blown off course by storms at some time in the distant past. Because there were few other birds on the desertlike Galápagos Islands, the finch colonists had plenty of space to set up house and little competition for food. Darwin suspected that the different beak shapes were part of a natural selection process. In any given area, the most successful birds would have been those whose beak size and shape helped them make use of whatever food was available: large seeds, small seeds, and so forth. Those birds passed along their beak type by reproducing, until eventually a particular beak type became common in that area. Over long stretches of time, Darwin suggested, descendants might become so different from their ancestors as to be considered new species. This kind of evolution accounts for the diversity of species we see on Earth today. (As Darwin knew, humans are able to re-create this process at a much faster rate through artificial selection, the selective breeding of plants and animals to bring out particular traits.)

If a species fails to evolve—if it fails to adapt to its environment—the result may be *extinction*, the death of every member of that species. Extinction sometimes occurs naturally, such as when a dramatic climate change happens too quickly for species to adapt. In other cases, extinction occurs because the species is forced out of its natural environment and is unable to find similar environment, or because all the individuals are killed by other species. Either way, extinction is final.

WHY CLASSIFY?

People have probably always found ways to tell the different kinds of animals and plants apart: those that run, fly, or swim; those that are edible versus those that are likely to eat you (or make you sick); and so forth.

In the mid-eighteenth century, a Swedish scientist named Carolus Linnaeus began sorting plants and animals into groups in an effort to reveal life's organizational "plan." Although Linnaeus was not the first person to attempt this, he was the first to sort species into larger categories to show their relationships. In naming species, he used easy-to-identify features, like leaf shape, scales, fur, and feathers, as guides. Each living thing was given two names: a *genus name* (general name) and a *species name* (a specific name not shared by any other member of the genus). Together, these two words define a species—just as your first and last names reveal both your individuality and your membership in a family.

Linnaeus's system, called *binomial nomenclature* (two-named naming system), is still in use today. It has been expanded into the science of *taxonomy*, which names species and sorts them into broader and broader groups based on the characteristics they share.

The other great advantage of taxonomy is that it crosses all language boundaries. Consider the beautiful orange and black monarch butterfly, which can be found from Canada to Mexico. In Spanish, the word for "butterfly" is *mariposa*. In Cherokee, it's *ka–ma–ma*. People in the French-speaking Canadian provinces call the butterfly *papillon*. Thanks to Linnaeus's system, however, there's just one taxonomic name for the monarch butterfly—*Danaus plexippus*—and it's understood by biologists all over the world.

FINDING THE THREADS

In taxonomy, the similarities between species are used to unite them within larger groups. Each genus belongs to a family, and families are subsets of orders. Orders fit into classes, and classes fit into phyla (the plural of *phylum*). The largest group is the kingdom, of which scientists currently recognize five: monerans (single-celled creatures), protists (microscopic single-celled or multicellular creatures), fungi, plants, and animals. The taxonomy of our monarch butterfly, *Danaus plexippus*, looks like this: Family Danaidae (milkweed butterflies), Order Lepidoptera (butterflies and moths), Class Insecta, Phylum Arthropoda (invertebrate animals with jointed bodies), Kingdom Animalia.

Unlike Linnaeus and other early scientists, modern biologists recognize that species change over time. They also know that appearance isn't always a reliable indicator of whether species are related. Organisms can sometimes look similar but have completely different origins. For example, sharks are fishes and dolphins are mammals. Modern scientists define a species as a group of individuals living in the wild who are able to mate and produce fertile offspring. Different species are considered relatives if they look or behave similarly, if their embryos (fertilized eggs) go through similar stages of development, or if the genetic makeup of their cells is similar—all of which suggest a shared ancestry.

Biologists do much more than name and sort organisms, of course. They seek to discover the history of life on Earth. *Systematics* is a method used to find evolutionary relationships between species. These relationships can be diagrammed in *clades*, or biological family trees. The base of the clade represents the ancestor of a particular group. Each branch off the "trunk" marks the evolution of a characteristic that resulted in either a new species or a whole new group of species. For the clade to be accurate, all species on a single branch must possess the new characteristic.

AN UNENDING CIRCLE

Invertebrates are constantly being discovered in out-of-the-way parts of the planet: in deep-sea vents, living on or in the bodies of other animals, burrowed in the sand, or floating in the open ocean. Their diversity helps us to discover how truly complex and beautiful the puzzle of life on Earth is and to see how all the pieces fit together.

CHAPTER TWO

S P O N G E S

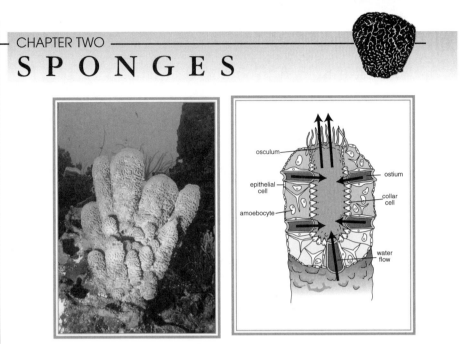

Sponges feed by filtering the seawater around them.
Water is drawn in by the beating of hairlike flagella inside
the sponge's hollow body cavity.

To most people, sponges are merely household tools, useful for washing the car and cleaning the house. Although most of the sponges we buy today are synthetic, or made from chemicals, natural sponges have been used by humans for thousands of years. Ancient Greeks used sponges to pad their armor, and Roman soldiers took advantage of the sponges' water-holding ability, using them like drinking cups. Egyptians gathered dead sponges from the seashore, and Greeks ancient and modern have braved deep dives to collect them.

Yet until the late 1700s, no one realized what these squishy objects really were: the "skeletons" of once-living animals.

PLANT OR ANIMAL?

An animal is defined as a multicellular life-form that gets its energy by eating other living things. Yet sponges seem to just sit there, showing no sign of feeding activity. Ancient people simply assumed that sponges were plants. But in the late 1700s scientists determined that sponges have none of the traits associated with plants—no roots, shoots, or leaves. The question then became: if sponges are animals, how do they feed themselves?

The mystery was solved when a biologist added colored dye to the water near a sponge. Suddenly, observers could see the movement of water around the sponge clearly. Dye streamed in through tiny pores, which are like pinpricks all over the sponge's surface. A short time later, colored water came streaming out the large, mouthlike opening at the top of the sponge. Apparently, the sponge didn't have to move because it could suck water and food right into itself like a living vacuum cleaner.

Water contains everything a sponge needs to survive. Bacteria and tiny, floating plants and animals, called *plankton*, are pulled into its body. Oxygen is absorbed from the surrounding water too. Water currents remove wastes from a sponge's body and, as researchers learned, also carry away its sperm, eggs, and *larvae* (immature offspring).

Once sponges were determined to be animals, biologists had to figure out where these odd creatures fit among the more familiar animal groups. The sponges' simple body plans and their process of development from egg to adult are so unusual that taxonomists created a new group just for them. Labeled as *parazoa* ("beside the animals"), sponges were placed on a separate branch at the base of the animal kingdom's family tree.

More than 900 species of sponges are known from the fossil record, dating back 700 million years. Of the species living today, about 5,000 have been named and studied, and there may be thousands more species living in difficult-to-reach corners of the world, where humans have yet to explore. Sponges probably evolved before other animals and have survived to live alongside them for millions of years, but no other types of animals have evolved from sponges.

In the animal kingdom, sponges are a bit of a puzzle. Every other kind of animal is made up of *tissues*—groups of specialized cells that work together to perform a single "job." Tissue types include muscle, skin, blood, and so on. Organs, such as the heart and liver, are tissues that manage the body's functions. The nervous system (brain, spinal cord, and nerves) is a network of cells that, together, coordinate movement and regulate the other tissues.

Sponges have no specialized tissues. Instead, their bodies are like bowls. A layer of cells covering the outside of the body is protective and contains the pores through which water enters the body. A second layer of cells lines the body cavity and works to filter food and remove wastes. A mass of soft material fills the space between these layers, contains special cells for reproduction and digestion and fibers that work like a skeleton. Each cell in a sponge's body has a particular task to do, and it does that task independently.

Sponges must live in water and need a hard surface to latch onto—but that's about where their specific requirements end. They thrive in the shallowest seas, but are equally at home in the murky waters over the continental shelves, where the seafloor slopes gradually into the deep ocean. About 150 sponge species live in freshwater lakes and streams. Some sponges can even endure the icy polar seas or live in the darkest depths of the ocean—down to 28,000 feet (8,537 meters) below sea level, where the cold and pressure would kill most creatures.

GETTING INSIDE A SPONGE

A living sponge doesn't resemble the synthetic sponges we use to bathe and clean. Instead, sponges look like soft-sided vases, narrow tubes, or formless blobs. Sponges can be as small as the tip of a shoelace or stand taller than a tall person. They come in a stunning range of colors, from silky brown to neon yellow to flowery purple.

Among some species, it's hard to tell one individual sponge from another. They grow together tightly like moss and can take over very large areas of the seafloor.

A layer of close-fitted, leathery cells forms the sponge's outer surface. Scattered between them are pores leading into narrow tunnels, or canals, that pierce the body wall. Water is drawn into them by the beating of hairlike *flagella* attached to cells inside the body of the sponge. One dime-size section of a sponge's body may contain thousands of these pore-and-canal systems.

Sponges don't move around in their environment, yet they do a tremendous amount of work. Studies have shown that in a single day, one teacup-size sponge can pump 1,321 gallons (5,000 liters) of water. The filtering activity of an entire colony creates a current that affects the environment all around it.

FOOD AND DRINK

Water loaded with floating food and oxygen enters a sponge's body through the thousands of canals, which empty into water-filled spaces deep inside the body.

Lining the hollow inside a sponge's body are millions of lightbulb-shaped *collar cells*. The rounded end of each collar cell is buried in the soft body wall, while its tip—shaped like a shirt collar—points into the open body cavity. Flagella extend from each collar cell into the watery chamber. The flagella beat back and forth, creating a powerful current that pulls tiny, floating morsels of food toward the body wall. Food particles become trapped on the sticky collars and are sucked inside. This wonderfully efficient system allows a sponge to gather about 90 percent of the food particles that pass through its body.

The "spongy" part of a sponge's body lies between the outer and inner cell layers. It's made of a jellylike material and has digestive, reproductive, and skeletal cells floating within it. Roving cells digest food particles and carry the nutrients to different parts of the body. Along the way, they move wastes to the inner cell wall and let them flow out into the surrounding water.

Roving cells also secrete the materials that form the sponge's skeleton. Although this skeleton is nothing like the bony one inside your body, it is vital to a sponge's survival. The skeletal fibers provide support so that the sponge doesn't collapse as it grows. They hold the canals open and, because they're sharp as needles, protect the sponge from predators.

SPONGE STYLES

The simplest sponges are shaped like bags, vases, or test tubes. Such sponges have thin, smooth body walls and a single central cavity. Slightly more advanced species have body walls that are folded into wrinkles and ridges. These folds increase the sponge's surface area, making room for more pores, canals, and collar cells and allowing the animal to collect water and food more rapidly.

The last group of sponges is even more complex. These have no central cavity. Instead, the body walls are thickened and dotted with many small chambers. Incoming canals twist and turn like mazes through these walls and into the chambers, where food is absorbed. Outgoing canals carry wastes out of the body.

STICK 'EM UP!

Sponges look like the easiest targets on Earth. They're soft, exposed, and unable to escape from danger or fight their attackers. Yet sponges have few predators. How can this be?

The answer lies inside a sponge's body wall. The tough fibers that form the skeleton also serve as a wickedly effective defense. Scientists group sponges into three classes, based on the chemical structure of their skeletal fibers. At least nine out of ten sponge species are classified as demosponges. Demosponge skeletons are built either of the soft protein spongin, or of sharp fibers called *spicules*. Some demosponges contain both. Spicules are like hardened snowflakes, bearing one to four pointed rays set at right angles to each other.

Calcareous sponges are named for calcium carbonate, the chalky chemical that forms their skeletons. Chalk spicules have three or four solid rays. Glass sponges, the third group, are more ancient and simpler than the other two classes but are equally well defended. Their skeletons, as the name suggests, are filled with glass spicules, each bearing six spikes. Whatever a sponge's skeleton is made of, when a predator takes a bite the effect is the same: a mouthful of sharp, painful fibers.

Some sponges have an additional weapon: poison. Such sponges are not usually deadly, but a predator who gets a taste doesn't soon forget the experience. Humans are as vulnerable to these poisons as are other animals. One touch of the fire sponge, for example, causes a nasty rash. But at the same time, researchers have discovered that a few of these chemicals may work as human medicines. Some affect the heart, digestion, or breathing. Others reduce inflammation, and a few work as antibiotics to fight infections.

Scientists are interested in another strange sponge survival skill as well: *regeneration*, or the ability to regrow body parts. Sponges can easily replace parts of themselves that get eaten or broken off. And their remarkable regenerative ability doesn't end there. If individual cells from a sponge are separated and then released into water, they move slowly across the bottom until they find one another. When cells from different species are released together, they can sort themselves correctly until eventually, one lump of cells forms for each species. Every cell-pile grows into a healthy, new sponge. No one knows how the cells recognize one another. Obviously, there's a lot more to sponges than meets the eye.

A SPONGE'S LIFE

Sponges can also use regeneration as a way to reproduce. Small stalks sprout like arms from the body of the parent sponge.

Eventually these stalks break off and float away to settle in a new location. This is a form of asexual reproduction because it occurs without the mixing of genes from two parents. A sponge produced this way is a *clone* that is genetically identical to its parent.

Freshwater sponges use asexual reproduction when their water sources begin to dry up. Before the parent sponge dies, it forms buds inside its body. These small packages of cells can survive on dry land, remaining *dormant* (in a state of suspended animation, like seeds) for a long time. The buds return to life again when they come in contact with water.

Other sponges start their lives just as you did—through the combination of a sperm cell from one parent and an egg cell from the other. Sponges don't come in male and female varieties, though. They alternate between the two, producing sperm for part of the year and eggs for the other. During its "male" phase, a sponge makes sperm in massive quantities, releasing the cells in dense clouds that float away on water currents. Most of these sperm die or become food for other animals, but a few always manage to reach other sponges, where they are sucked in through the pores.

Once inside another sponge's body, sperm are captured by collar cells just like any other bit of floating debris. Fortunately, the collar cells recognize sperm as something other than food. The collar cells now become transport cells, carrying sperm through the body wall to the eggs. Fertilized eggs develop quickly into hollow, ball-like larvae covered in short flagella, which the larvae use like oars. Larvae are released into the sponge's body cavity and paddle off into the surrounding water.

A larva's floating freedom is short-lived. It will soon fall to the bottom of its ocean, river, or lake to face adulthood. Once settled, the larva undergoes a *metamorphosis*, or change in body shape and function. The young sponge literally turns inside-out, so its flagella face inward around the edges of a hollow space. Each cell with attached flagella becomes a collar cell.

Sponges form an important part of reef communities, alongside sea anemones, corals, tube worms, nudibranchs, crabs, and other marine organisms. Colorful microscopic algae live inside the cells of some sponges.

FRIENDS AND NEIGHBORS

Sponges don't live in isolation. In fact, they often provide homes for a wide variety of other sea creatures. Sponges in southern Australia live side-by-side with corals and a variety of other beautiful and colorful creatures, including sea anemones, spiral tube worms, nudibranchs (sea slugs), and sea urchins. Small crabs and sea stars climb around on the sponges, gathering algae or seeking unsuspecting prey. Many of the species living in these sponge gardens can't be found anywhere else in the world.

Small marine (saltwater) plants make their homes around the pores of some sponges, while bacteria and algae may live inside a sponge's cells. These microscopic guests are often the source of the brilliant colors sponges exhibit. *Symbiotic* relationships like these benefit both species—the microorganisms are supported and protected by their host sponges, while the sponges can feed on the waste products of their guests. Sponges may have had this kind of relationship with blue-green algae for 650 million years.

In another unusual relationship, some hermit crabs use sponges as portable *camouflage* (a form of concealment that helps the animal blend into its environment). A hermit crab usually tucks

Exploring Sponge Reefs

In the summer of 1999, Canadian and German scientists joined forces for an exceptional adventure: to explore the world's only known living glass-sponge reef.

Squeezed inside the submersible vehicle *Delta,* researchers descended 800 feet (244 meters) into the waters over British Columbia's continental shelf, where the North American landmass slopes gently into the Pacific Ocean. To their amazement, glass sponges covered over 386 square miles (1,000 square kilometers) of seafloor. The reef probably began to grow when glaciers from the last Ice Age melted, about 10,000 years ago, and the Pacific Ocean became warmer and deeper.

Although this is the only living glass-sponge reef known today, fossils suggest that the warm climate 200 million years ago was perfectly suited for them. One ancient reef began in North America and extended 4,340 miles (7,000 kilometers) across the Atlantic Ocean, through the Mediterranean Sea, and into the Black Sea, near Romania. Another, off the coast of Spain, grew to be 230 feet (70 meters) thick and at least 496 miles (800 kilometers) long.

Generation after generation, living sponges grow atop the hard, fused skeletons of sponges that lived and died before them. Today, some British Columbian sponges tower 49 feet (15 meters) or more above the seafloor, providing an important *habitat* for other bottom-dwelling invertebrates and juvenile fish.

itself inside the abandoned shell of a sea snail, carrying the shell around on its back for protection. Crabs in the genus *Pagarus*, however, often collect sponges to cover the surfaces of their chosen shell-homes. When the sponge becomes too heavy to carry, the crab comes out and digs a hole in the sponge, living there until it finds a new shell.

STRANGE AND WONDERFUL

Despite their simplicity, sponges have lived on Earth for 700 million years, perhaps 50 million years longer than any other group of animals. Though some sponge species died off during Earth's five *mass extinctions*—times in our planet's history when dramatic environmental changes caused large numbers of species to die off quickly—as a group they have survived remarkably well. (The last mass extinction, 65 million years ago, killed off the dinosaurs. Another, 250 million years ago, resulted in the extinction of more than 90 percent of the animal species in Earth's oceans.)

Sponges provide a good reminder that evolution doesn't always work to make living things more complex. Most of the time, evolution simply "molds" living things bit by bit, until their bodies and behavior work in harmony with their environments. Then, so long as the environments don't change, species can remain as they are. Apparently, sponges found their "harmony" long ago.

CHAPTER THREE

J E L L I E S

"Jelly" is a common name that includes many species of cnidarians—jellyfishes, box jellyfishes, hydrae, sea anemones, corals, and others—as well as ctenophores, better known as comb jellies.

What strange creatures jellies are! Practically transparent, they spend their lives floating on water currents or anchored to the bottoms of oceans, rivers, and lakes. Their bodies, shaped like bowls, cups, or hot-air balloons, are fringed with armlike *tentacles* that wave freely in the water in search of food.

WHAT'S A CNIDARIAN?

One of the best places to meet cnidarians is along the seashore, where they often wash up with the tide. Stranded on the sand, a jelly looks as harmless as a plastic bag full of water. But don't touch! The tentacles of jellyfishes and other cnidarians are lined with stinging cells that can cause a painful rash or allergic reaction.

Near the shore, swimmers and divers often meet jellyfishes floating on the waves. Sea anemones may look like blooming, green flowers clinging to the sides of rocky tide pools. Hydrae and corals are small jellies that anchor themselves to the bottom and rarely move at all. In warm, tropical waters, corals form massive reefs that grow over large sections of the seabed.

Some jellies are so small that they're hardly visible without a microscope. Others are almost unimaginably large—the lion's mane jellyfish, for example, has a body 7.9 feet (2.5 meters) wide with tentacles that may extend 120 feet (37 meters).

THE LIFE OF A JELLY

Whatever their size or shape, cnidarians share a fascinating life history. Instead of being born as small versions of their parents, cnidarians hatch from their eggs in one body shape, then metamorphose into another form when they reach adulthood. Most jellies alternate between two forms: *medusa* and *polyp*.

Medusae have the familiar jellyfish shape, with wide bodies (called "bells") that resemble open umbrellas. The medusa's mouth is located at the bottom of the bell, and its tentacles trail below it. Medusae are wanderers, floating freely or swimming gently in water currents. Polyps look like upside-down medusae, attached to the bottoms of shallow lakes, rivers, and seas. A suction-cuplike sucker on the bell anchors the polyp in place, and its mouth and tentacles point upward to grab food floating by.

These two body plans confused scientists for hundreds of years. Aristotle, an ancient Greek philosopher and naturalist, assumed they were different species. Linnaeus wasn't convinced that jellies were animals at all. By the 1800s, scientists had learned that polyps and medusae are different stages in the lives of the same animals. And although Aristotle didn't get the classification of jellies quite right, he did contribute to their naming. The word "cnidaria" is a tribute to his description of the polyp—*knide* is Greek for "nettle," a kind of sharp, stinging burr found on some plants.

MEET THE JELLIES

Taxonomists class cnidarians based on their form—polyp or medusa—as adults. True jellyfish are in the class Scyphozoa. Most young jellyfishes start life as polyps but spend their adulthood in the medusa form. Those that live in the open ocean, however, where delicate polyps can't reach the deep seafloor, live out their whole lives as medusae.

Class Cubozoa includes the box jellyfishes, which look and live much like regular jellyfishes, except that their bodies are more squarely shaped. The bell has flat sides instead of the rounded edges found in true jellies. To humans, box jellies are the most deadly cnidarians of all. The sea wasp, *Chironex fleckeri*, is responsible for the deaths of more people in Australia than are sharks and crocodiles combined.

The class Anthozoa contains some of the most decorative and lovely cnidarians—corals, sea anemones, sea fans, and sea pens. These creatures spend their whole lives as polyps. Anthozoans that live in shallow, warm water are often colorful, thanks to the presence of symbiotic algae living inside their cells. Both organisms benefit from the relationship: algae that live inside jellies are safe from predators and release waste products that the jellies can use as food. In warm water, corals are colonial. Millions of individual polyps build hard shells around themselves and live side-by-side, constructing large reefs.

You already may have met a member of the class Hydrozoa in your science classroom. The hydra is a tiny, solitary polyp often found in rivers and lakes. Many students find hydrae when observing pond water under a microscope. The fire coral is another hydrozoan. These are not true corals, but they build a hard cup around themselves as do corals. The fire coral's name comes both from its coral-like shell and from the burning sting the animal inflicts when touched. Another famous hydrozoan is the Portuguese man-of-war. Often called a jellyfish, the man-of-war is actually a massive colony of hydrozoans, containing a mix of medusae and polyps. Each member of the colony is specialized for reproduction, feeding, stinging, or some other task.

SIMPLE WONDERS

Like sponges, cnidarians have no stomach or intestine. Food enters the body though a tube-shaped opening hidden between the tentacles. This "mouth" leads into a large body cavity, where digestive juices begin the breakdown of food into smaller particles. Digestion continues within the food vacuoles of individual cells.

Sea anenomes and jellyfishes are different forms of cnidarians. Sea anemones are polyps that live attached to the seafloor. Young jellyfishes are also polyps but become medusae as adults, floating freely on water currents.

Nutrients are transported throughout the cnidarian's body in canals that stretch across the bell like the spokes of a bicycle wheel.

Also like sponges, cnidarians collect oxygen from the water in a very simple manner: oxygen molecules can pass right through their skin. Waste products also cross through the skin, moving from the body into the water.

Beyond these shared traits, cnidarians have made some significant evolutionary gains over sponges. Unlike sponges, which have no organized body plans and may be asymmetrical (without balance in their body shapes), cnidarians have some symmetry. When observed from the top or bottom, a cnidarian looks like a child's drawing of the Sun—the round bell is fringed by tentacles that are evenly spaced like rays around the body's edge. Canals extending outward from the body cavity cut the bell into even sections, like slices of pie.

Animals (except for sponges) can be divided into two groups based on body symmetry: those that have *radial symmetry* (are sym-

Sea stars have radial symmetry as adults.

metrical around a central point) and those that have *bilateral symmetry* (have identical body halves). Cnidarians and ctenophores have radial symmetry, while most other animals—including humans—have bilateral symmetry. Echinoderms (sea stars and their relatives) are an interesting exception to the rule. They have bilateral symmetry as larvae and radial symmetry as adults.

HAVE A TISSUE

Cnidarians are the most ancient animals to have tissues—cells that work together to perform a particular body function. Jellies, like all the animals that evolved after them, have three layers of cells. In jellies, the *epidermis* (or skin) covers the outside of the body, the *gastrodermis* lines the hollow body cavity, and the *mesoglea* is sandwiched between. The mesoglea gives "jellies" their common name—it's a soft and cushiony mass that resembles gelatin.

Cnidarians don't have internal organs like you do, nor do they have a head or brain. But they've got nerves, muscles, and a mass of stringy cells that work like a skeleton. Nerves, scattered in a weblike network throughout the epidermis, work with muscles to help jellies respond to their environments. Some jellies even have special cells that detect motion and light. Distributed evenly around the body, these sensory cells allow cnidarians to respond to dangers from any direction. Other cells on the rim of the bell help the sightless cnidarians tell up from down.

ON THE MOVE

Most of the time, medusae use little or no energy to swim. Because their bodies are almost the exact density of water, jellies float along as if they themselves were pure liquid. When necessary, jellyfishes can swim and control their direction of movement.

A jellyfish swims by contracting muscles around the edges of its bell. With every pumping motion, the mesoglea is compressed (squeeze a water balloon and you'll get a similar effect). Water shoots out of the bell like air from a jet plane's engine and propels the jelly forward. To control its direction of movement, the jellyfish can contract some muscles while leaving others relaxed. Putting pressure on different sections of the mesoglea causes jellies to "lean" in one direction or another.

In humans and other vertebrates, muscles attach to a hard, internal skeleton. For vertebrates to move, the muscles must press or pull against these bones. Crabs, insects, and other shelled invertebrates move by contracting muscles attached between segments of their hard, external skeletons. Jellies, however, have no hard parts for their muscles to work against. Instead, the mesoglea is their source of support. Called a *hydrostatic* (water-stabilized) *skeleton*, this system works by enclosing body fluids inside a living "envelope." Like the water inside a water balloon, the mesoglea works to "pump up" the cnidarian, giving it shape and structure and providing a surface against which muscles can press to create movement.

Many jellyfish species, as well as the Portuguese man-of-war, can also move by "sailing." Large, open spaces under the bell fill with gases, catching the wind as the animal floats at the water's surface.

A Seamless Defense

One of the special characteristics of jellies is their method of food-capture and defense. Long tentacles extend from the bell like floppy arms. Jellies may have just a few tentacles or, in the case of box jellies, as many as sixty. Each tentacle is lined with thousands of special cells, each of which contains a stinging capsule called a *nematocyst*.

Whether the jelly is a polyp or medusa, its nematocysts are activated the same way—by touch. When the tentacles come in contact with anything solid, the nematocyst capsules burst open and a coiled thread shoots out. Some of these threads are specialized to grab or hold prey. Others have sharply pointed stingers, which quickly inject *toxins* to immobilize prey or to cause pain to predators. Among humans, these toxins may cause only a rash or welts on the skin. But some jellies produce toxins strong enough to cause heart and lung failure, or even death. Even a dead jelly washed up on the beach or a single tentacle separated from the cnidarian's body can inflict a sting.

Despite their nasty reputation, most cnidarians are completely harmless to humans, and some have no stinging cells at all. Instead, their poisons are meant to subdue small, floating invertebrates. After the jelly's prey is stung into submission, the meal is transferred to a set of short arms on the underside of the bell. These, in turn, lift food toward the bell and into the mouth.

Polyps tend to move as little as possible. Corals, hydrae, and anemones choose a spot and hold on tightly with their sucker-disks. When threatened, polyps pull their tentacles inside and make themselves into soft blobs that are hard to see. Hydrae and anemones, however, can move when necessary, and they're surprisingly acrobatic. Anemones swim by launching themselves into the water and bending their bodies backward and forward. Hydrae do cartwheel-like flips.

ALTERNATION OF GENERATIONS

As complex as their life cycles may be, cnidarian polyps sometimes use a very simple process to reproduce: they make copies of themselves. Buds grow like little branches from the body of the parent. When the buds are large enough, they break off and can survive on their own. These new jellies, produced asexually, are clones of the polyp from which they came. By "recycling" genetic material that's already been proven successful, one individual can quickly take over an area, producing copies of itself as the colonists.

Cnidarians also reproduce sexually through the mixing of sperm and eggs. Jellyfishes provide a good example. Each adult jellyfish, in its medusa form, is either male or female. Jellyfishes release their reproductive cells—sperm or eggs—into the water, where they meet randomly. Fertilized eggs develop into tiny larvae, which look like flattened footballs covered in tiny hairs.

A larva floats along in the water for a while and then settles to the bottom as a polyp. Jellyfish polyps reproduce asexually, as we've already seen. They bud off polyps, which settle to the bottom near their parents, or produce medusae, which float away to continue the cycle.

Like sponges, cnidarians have the ability to regenerate portions of their bodies. Jellyfishes often lose tentacles, for example, either through natural wear and tear or when a predator attacks. Regeneration is merely another form of asexual reproduction in which part of the body is reproduced.

FACING DANGER

Cnidarians defend themselves well and are excellent survivors. Corals have been around for more then 650 million years, as shown by the fossilized reefs they've left behind.

Jellies do have a few predators, though. Crown-of-thorns sea stars consume corals, and parrotfishes have "beaks" specially equipped with sharp teeth for crunching hard bits of coral reef.

Jellyfishes are a favorite food of many sea turtles and nudibranchs (sea slugs), which seem immune to the stings. Nudibranchs may even store the nematocysts in their bodies and use them as protection against their own predators. And at least one cnidarian species is cannibalistic. In the spring of 2000, a population of pink Caribbean jellyfishes was discovered in the Gulf of Mexico, far north of their usual feeding and breeding area, eating up the resident moon jellyfishes.

Sea anemones living along the shoreline not only have to worry about hungry nudibranchs, but they must also defend themselves against the dangers of low tide. To stay moist when exposed to air and sun, an anemone may shrivel up into a tight "stump" with its tentacles tucked inside. Some anemones pluck up bits of light-colored shell or rock and stick them to their bodies. These adornments reflect light to keep the animal cool and provide camouflage at the same time.

Anemones have also been known to defend their sections of the seafloor against intruders. The intertidal zone, where the ocean meets the shore, is one of the most active and densely populated regions of the sea. Space is hard to come by. Sea anemones protect their real estate by reaching out their tentacles and whacking neighbors with a stinging punch. A beaten anemone, or one that feels too threatened, will often let go of its rock and move to a new locale.

MAKING FRIENDS

In nature, jellies have a number of fascinating "friendships," or symbioses, with other species.

Brilliant orange-and-yellow-striped clownfishes spend their lives, from egg to adulthood, right among the tentacles of sea anemones. A layer of mucus on the little fishes' skin makes them immune to the anemone's stinging cells. Crabs and shrimp may

The stinging tentacles of sea anemones provide a safe haven for clownfish. In return for this protection, the clownfish keeps its anemone partner clean and provides it with food.

also wander around on anemones, their hard shells protecting them from stings.

Corals have partnerships, too, although you have to look a little closer to find them. Corals are naturally white or transparent, yet reefs are marked by splashy colors. This color comes from algae living inside the bodies of the coral animals. Algae are filled with *pigments* (light-absorbing chemicals) that help them collect sunlight, which is converted to energy through photosynthesis. A coral may host more than a million algae per square inch (6.5 square centimeters) of its body mass.

Although coral reefs are lush habitats, the waters around them are almost barren of life, containing very little plankton or bacteria. Oddly enough, the health of the reef depends on these lifeless waters: algae require clean, brilliantly clear water in order to photosynthesize well, and corals rely entirely on the waste products of their algae for food. It's a remarkable system but one

Worlds of Color

Coral reefs create some of the most ecologically diverse habitats on Earth. The Great Barrier Reef, off eastern Australia, is the largest of these. Although it's "only" half a million years old, the reef has grown to a length of almost 1,250 miles (2,011 kilometers), taking over an area of the ocean floor only slightly smaller than California. The Great Barrier Reef is actually made up of 2,900 separate reefs built by more than 350 species of coral. It is home to about 2,000 species of fishes, 4,000 kinds of mollusks (shelled invertebrates), 400 species of sponges, and countless other ocean going animals.

A reef starts when individual coral polyps settle on the bare ocean floor. Each polyp secretes a chalky substance that thickens into a hard shell. This shell is open at the top, allowing the polyp's tentacles to reach out for food. Thousands of polyps set up house side by side, their shells fusing together to form a solid mass. As corals die, new individuals build atop the empty shells. In this way, the reef grows upward off the bottom. Parts of the Great Barrier Reef tower 590 feet (180 meters) above the seafloor—the height of a fifty-nine-story building!

Each coral colony takes on a distinctive shape, depending on its species. There's one that looks just like a brain. The staghorn coral forms spiked arms that resemble a deer's antlers. Other species look like vases, broccoli, or even clusters of grapes.

that's easily disturbed. In some tropical areas, pollution muddies the waters and prevents sunlight from reaching the coral-algae partners. When the algae and corals die, many other plants and animals are affected, and a whole reef may be lost.

DON'T FORGET THE COMB JELLIES

Since 1671, sailors have reported seeing shimmering lights on the open ocean late at night. These lights are not magical, as early sailors believed, but are produced by ctenophores, which (like cnidarians) drift on wind and water currents.

The world's eighty known species of ctenophores, or comb jellies, are ocean dwellers that look remarkably like cnidarians. They have see-through, bell-shaped bodies and two dangling tentacles. Despite their similarities to other jellies, comb jellies don't have alternating life stages as do cnidarians. The life histories of comb jellies are so unlike those of the cnidarians, in fact, that scientists place them in a separate phylum. Ctenophores stay in the medusa form all their lives. They don't seem to reproduce asexually, and their eggs hatch into larvae that look like miniatures of the adults.

Eight straight rows of hairlike *cilia* run from the top of the comb jelly's bell to its bottom edge. Steady up-and-down beating of the cilia on these "combs" creates water currents that propel the animal gracefully through the water. The blue and green lights that captured the attention of sailors so long ago is produced by a chemical called luciferin that gives off energy in the form of light—rather like the chemical reaction that takes place in a neon sign. The cilia catch this light, reflecting it along the comb rows like rainbows and producing a dancing light show even in the dark of night.

Comb jellies are usually small, but together they eat more plankton than any other type of animal in the ocean. Though ctenophores have no stingers, their tentacles are lined with suckerlike cells that hold onto small prey like glue.

ONWARD AND UPWARD

Cnidarians and ctenophores, like sponges, have survived on Earth for hundreds of millions of years and have pioneered some remarkable innovations. These innovations, including three cell layers, body symmetry, and true tissues, paved the way for the evolution of more complex animals.

CHAPTER FOUR

FLATWORMS

True to their names, flatworms are as flat as pancakes and are made to glide like living waves through water and damp soil. Some of these worms even live their lives within the bodies of other animals.

MIRROR IMAGES

We started by investigating sponges, which have only two layers of cells, no tissues, and no particular organization to their body shape. Next came the jellies—cnidarians and ctenophores—that have true tissues and bodies organized tidily around a central point.

Flatworms are the next step up in body organization. Their bodies not only contain tissues; they have bilateral symmetry. Draw a line down the length of the worm's body and you'll see that each side is a mirror image of the other. At one end you'll find a head. At the opposite end, you'll find a tail. Now take a look in the mirror. While you're larger and more complex, your body is arranged in the same way. All of the species that evolved after flatworms share this type of symmetry (although sea stars and their relatives are only bilaterally symmetrical as larvae).

SORTING THROUGH THE FLATWORMS

Flatworms make up the phylum Platyhelminthes. Many of the approximately 20,000 flatworm species are *parasites*, using the tissues of other organisms as their sources of food and shelter.

Sorting out the evolutionary history of flatworms is a difficult process because a flatworm's body contains almost nothing that's hard enough to fossilize. Instead, flatworm species are classified based on their body shape and their way of life: free-living flatworms, flukes, and tapeworms.

The little, shovel-headed planarians, which live in water or soil, and the fringed marine polyclads are among the flatworms often

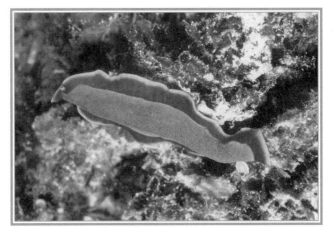

Bright skin colors warn predators that marine flatworms are poisonous (or are mimicking the color patterns of poisonous sea slugs).

referred to as free-living because they don't make their homes on or in other animals. Free-living flatworms are generally quite small—from less than 1/50 inch (0.05 millimeters) to about 1 foot (30 centimeters) in length and a fraction of an inch (or centimeter) in thickness.

Flukes are also small, with teardrop-or cylinder-shaped bodies. Flukes are parasites that attach themselves to the internal organs of other animals and are major causes of disease in people and animals worldwide.

The last group is the tapeworms. You've probably used a tape measure—a long piece of fabric or metal with inches and/or centimeters marked along its length. Now imagine a tape measure that's built of many segments, each of an equal length and hooked together end-to-end like the cars on a train. That's the basic body plan of an adult tapeworm. Long and segmented, tapeworms live inside the intestine of vertebrates. The fish tapeworm is perhaps the longest, growing up to 82 feet (25 meters) in length.

Flatworms go through several life stages, including eggs, larvae, and adults. Parasitic worms rely on two or three host species and go through several larval stages to complete their life cycle from egg to adulthood.

Flatworm Beauty Queens

Before you get the impression that all flatworms are creepy beasts, take a look at the polyclads. You might easily mistake a polyclad for a colorful leaf lying on the seabed. These marine flatworms are shaped like tiny oval tablecloths, with flaps of skin forming soft ruffles around their sides. Many polyclads have almost transparent skin through which all their internal organs can be seen clearly. Algae often live inside polyclads, lending bright colors to their wormy hosts. Other polyclads create their own color patterns. Some are lemon-yellow with bold, black spots. Some are marked in white, orange, and black like a leopard. Still others bear bands of color that circle the body like the rings on a dartboard.

Such bright color patterns, called *warning coloration,* are often found in poisonous animals. Indeed, some polyclads do produce toxic chemicals. Although these chemicals probably aren't strong enough to kill, they leave a bad taste in a predator's mouth that isn't soon forgotten. Fishes have excellent color vision and quickly learn to avoid bad-tasting or dangerous prey.

Most brightly colored polyclads aren't poisonous, however. Instead, their color patterns mimic those of other invertebrates such as nudibranchs (sea slugs), which truly are toxic. Predators mistake the polyclads for dangerous nudibranchs and stay away.

LINKS TO THE PAST

Despite all their advancements, flatworms still have a lot in common with their cnidarian ancestors. For example, both obtain oxygen by absorbing it through their skin. This is where a flatworm's flatness comes in handy. Because a flat worm's body is so thin, every cell in it is close to its surrounding environment.

Oxygen moves easily from the water, across the flatworm's skin, and into its body. As a result, flatworms don't need lungs, gills, or hearts.

When it comes to digestion, flatworms and jellies have another trait in common: a pocket-shaped digestive tract with a single opening, located on the belly. Food comes in through this mouth and wastes are expelled from it. The internal body cavity of a flatworm is more complex than that of a jelly, though. The cavity branches to extend in all directions, so nutrients reach every part of the animal's body.

Flatworms, like jellies and sponges, have hydrostatic skeletons. Body fluids held under pressure by an envelope of skin work as a solid surface against which muscles can press.

A FEEL FOR THE WORLD

Flatworms have the most complex system of muscles we've seen so far. It is arranged in three separate layers. One layer runs up and down the length of the worm, while another is organized in rings around the worm's body. A third set of muscles angles diagonally across the body. Together, these muscle groups make flatworms flexible and strong. Additionally, cilia cover the skin of a flatworm's belly and sides like a lush carpet. When a flatworm moves, the cilia wave back and forth like miniature swimming arms. At the same time, waves of muscle contractions, starting at the tail and swelling toward the head, provide pushing and pulling movements that scoot the animal headfirst through its environment.

Flatworms are also equipped with many types of cells that help them sense and respond to the world around them. Flatworms have a simple type of brain, called a *cerebral ganglion*, made up of a collection of nerve cells. Nerve cords run like a two-lane road from this ganglion down the length of the body, transmitting signals from the brain to the body and back again. A flatworm gets its "feel for the world" through receptors on its head and body, which sense movement in the surrounding environment. Also scattered across the worm's skin are chemical receptors. Worms locate food and mates by picking up chemical "scent trails" in the water.

If you look through a microscope, one or more pairs of eyespots on the flatworm's head seem to be staring right back up at you. Flatworms can't see images as you do, but their eyespots are sensitive to light. Many species also grow tentacles on their heads, which function like outstretched arms to extend the worms' sense of touch, like a cat's whiskers.

LIFESTYLES OF THE FLAT AND SQUIRMY

There's almost nothing familiar about the lifestyles of flatworms. Most people wouldn't imagine that such small and primitive creatures have much of a life story at all. But that couldn't be farther from the truth. Flatworms have so many approaches to feeding and reproduction that libraries full of books have been written about them. Some scientists dedicate their whole careers to the study of flatworms, and health workers worldwide are fascinated by them as well.

TWO PERFECT HOSTS

To see what all the fuss is about, let's take a close look at the life cycle of one of the most widespread flatworm parasites, the blood fluke *Schistosoma*. These flukes infect at least 200 million people in tropical countries worldwide, causing symptoms ranging from fever and weight loss to permanent intestinal, lung, and liver damage.

It begins with a single fluke, nestled happily near the bile ducts of a human host's liver. The adult fluke, rarely more than 0.4 inches (1 centimeter) long, can live for many years. The worm uses a rough-edged sucker on its mouth both as an anchor and as a feeding utensil. It's a convenient set up, rather like a human living with a straw in its mouth, sucking on a bottomless chocolate milkshake.

Every fluke has both male and female sex organs, but produces sperm and eggs at different times. As many as 3,000 eggs are fertilized and released daily into the host's bloodstream. They burrow through the intestinal wall and exit the body in the feces. Out in the world, blood fluke eggs are transported far and wide when human feces is flushed into rivers or lakes or spread onto fields and gardens as fertilizer, or passed along when people don't wash their hands. The results can be disastrous.

As soon as fluke eggs are exposed to water, they hatch into swimming larvae. A larva has only one day to locate a freshwater snail, its second host. The swimmer burrows through the snail's skin and sets up camp in its digestive gland. At this stage, fluke larvae can reproduce asexually, simply by splitting themselves in half. This process continues for several weeks, allowing a single fluke to produce up to 250,000 copies of itself. These larvae swim out of the snail's body in search of people bathing or working in the water.

Getting into a human host is merely a matter of boring through its skin. Larvae find their way into the bloodstream, which carries them right to the liver. Then the cycle is complete and begins again.

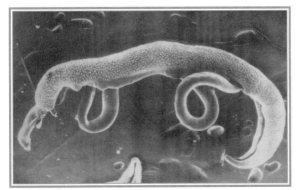

The blood fluke *Schistosoma* infects over 200 million people worldwide. It spreads in the presence of unsanitary conditions, such as when human feces is flushed into water sources.

Recycling Flatworms

Flatworms take regeneration to far greater extremes than any of the animals we've met so far.

Flatworms often use regeneration to reproduce asexually. Their bodies split down the middle, and then missing body parts are regrown on each half—the head-half grows a tail, and the tail-half grows a head. Flatworms also use regeneration as a way of replacing lost or damaged body parts, as do sponges and cnidarians. Yet planarians, those tiny, free-living flatworms, can survive being cut into as many as thirty-two parts. Each piece grows into a healthy, new worm.

When your skin is cut, new cells grow around the edges of the wound. Your muscles and skin heal in one solid piece, looking much as they did before the injury.

If lengthwise cuts are made in the tail or head of a planarian, however, there's a different result. The planarian heals its cuts too, but instead of stitching the damaged ends back together, new cells grow to close up each section. If a planarian's tail is cut into ten segments, when the animal heals it will have ten tails.

Although flatworm regeneration has been studied in great detail, scientists are still sorting out the exact process that makes it possible. Researchers have learned that when cuts are made, healing begins within fifteen minutes. Ten to fourteen days later, the injury is completely healed. The source of this rapid regeneration may be *neoblasts*, special cells that can multiply and develop into any other kind of body cell.

HUNGRY WORMS

The search for food takes up much of the day for most animals, and flatworms are no exception. One of the fascinating aspects of flatworm biology is the variety of ways in which they feed.

Free-living flatworms may begin their lives as *herbivores* (plant-eaters), munching algae off rocks or catching swimming diatoms, which are glassy, planktonic (floating) creatures that are common in salt water. Adult planarians and polyclads are usually *carnivores* (flesh-eaters), swimming slowly over the bottom or ducking into cracks and crevices in search of invertebrate prey. A few species are *scavengers*, which are like natural garbage collectors—they eat the bodies of dead animals and, in so doing, clean up their local environments.

Some free-living flatworms have algae or other microscopic, plantlike creatures living within their bodies. Flatworms in the genus *Convoluta* are only 1/25 to 1/8 of an inch (1 to 3 millimeters) long and are barely visible without a microscope—yet each tiny individual may have as many as 25,000 algae inside its tissues. The algae "stain" their hosts a brilliant green. When large groups of *Convoluta* gather in shallow water or on shorelines, it's as if neon-green paint has been poured into the water. Blue-green algae use their pigments to photosynthesize as plants do, collecting sunlight and converting it to energy. Algae can also make use of the nitrogen-based waste products in the flatworm's body. In turn, algae provide oxygen and sugars that help feed the worm.

LIVING THE EASY LIFE

Parasitic flatworms need not hunt, because their food can be found right in front of their faces. Both flukes and tapeworms live inside the bodies of other animals and remain attached to hosts throughout adulthood.

An adult fluke or tapeworm latches onto the wall of its host's intestine or to some other internal organ. Sharp hooks around the worm's mouth help it stay firmly attached. A layer of exceptionally thick skin, called a *cuticle*, surrounds the parasite's body, providing protection from the digestive enzymes and other harsh chemicals often produced by the host's organs.

Flukes feed on the host's body tissues or blood, or collect partially digested materials from the stomach. Many flukes "spit out" digestive chemicals onto the part of the host's body they want to eat. This softens the tissues and makes them easier to consume.

Tapeworms live in the intestine of their hosts. The tapeworm has absolutely no organs for digestion—it does not even have a mouth. Surrounded on all sides by its food source, the tapeworm simply absorbs food particles across its skin in much the same way that oxygen is collected by flatworms living in water.

THE POETRY OF FLATWORMS

You're not alone if you look at flatworms and wonder, "What use are they?" Most are far from beautiful, and many have lifestyles strange enough to make you shiver. The poetry of these worms— the source of their charm and wonder (for biologists, anyway)—lies in their very strangeness and the questions they inspire. How did flukes and tapeworms learn to survive inside the bodies of other animals? What brought about their incredibly complex life cycles? The dazzling coloration of polyclads and the simple elegance of planarians are equally confusing, standing in stark contrast to their alienlike, parasitic cousins.

The evolutionary breakthroughs pioneered by these worms are quite impressive: a much more organized nervous system, bilateral symmetry, and the presence of a distinct head and tail. These traits not only added to the complexity of animals as a group, but also provided a framework within which a greater variety of animals could evolve.

CHAPTER FIVE

RIBBON WORMS,
ROUNDWORMS, AND ROTIFERS

You're not alone if you've never heard of roundworms, ribbon worms, or rotifers. Most of these worms, and many of Earth's other wormlike creatures, are so small that people never know of their existence, even though they occur in huge numbers right in our own backyards.

LIVING RIBBONS

If you thought flatworms were odd, wait until you meet the ribbon worms of Phylum Nemertea. Visit the beach and you'll find ribbon worms tucked under rocks or among plants and seaweed in shallow water. You'll recognize them by their long, shoestringlike shape and brilliantly colored bodies. They range in color from creamy white to green, orange, purple, or pink. Some are even striped like candy canes. Ribbon worms feed by sticking sharp-tipped tubes out of their mouths with which they spear or lasso their prey. The tip of this spear, which scientists call a *proboscis*, is sometimes loaded with toxins powerful enough to paralyze a shrimp or worm but is not dangerous to humans.

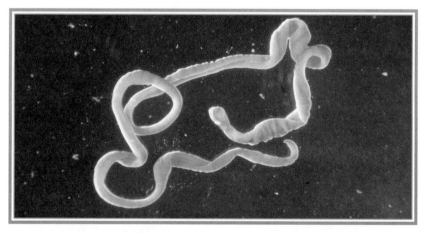

Ribbon worms were the first animals to have a one-way digestive tract, allowing them to eat and digest at the same time.

Ribbon worms may be a small group, only containing about 900 species, but they are very important. Ribbon worm were the first organisms to have one-way digestive tracts. Food enters through the worm's mouth and then is digested in a series of pockets inside the intestine. Wastes, instead of being expelled through the mouth as in the simpler animals we've seen so far, are removed from the opposite end, through an anus.

That might not sound terribly exciting, but for evolutionary biologists it's a revelation. Ribbon worms were the first animals to have this kind of straight-through digestive tract. With it, these revolutionary creatures could eat a meal while still digesting the last one. Like their flatworm ancestors, ribbon worms are free-living animals usually found in salt water. Unlike the flatworms, however, which are rarely even 1 foot (30 centimeters) long, ribbon worms may reach lengths of 98 feet (30 meters). It's their ability to eat almost constantly that allows for such impressive growth.

Yet another innovation is found among the ribbon worms: a *circulatory system* to transport oxygenated blood throughout the animal's body. A ribbon worm's circulatory system contains no heart. Instead, a special set of muscles pumps blood through a network of tube-shaped vessels. Oxygen is carried in the blood by red blood cells similar to the ones in your own blood.

LIVING THREADS

Roundworms make up the phylum Nematoda, which means "threadlike." That's an accurate description of these creatures, which are usually much longer than they are wide and are pointed at each end. Despite our unfamiliarity with them, nematode worms form one of the most diverse animal phyla. About 12,000 roundworm species have been named, but as many as 200,000 species may exist. There are sometimes thousands of individual roundworms in a single cup of soil, sand, or water. Nematodes are a real success story, evolving more than 300 million years ago.

A lot of research has been done on roundworms because many of them are parasites. Hookworms, pinworms, heartworms, and *Ascaris*, an intestinal parasite, are roundworms commonly found in humans, pets, and domestic animals such as horses and cattle. Many live in soil and as parasites on plants. Other roundworms are at home in some of the most extreme habitats Earth has to offer, including hot springs and polar ice.

A WORMY WAY OF LIFE

Roundworms, like ribbon worms, have quite an advanced digestive system based on a hollow, one-way tube that runs through the center of the animal's body. When a roundworm eats a bacterial cell, takes a bite of another worm, or munches some decaying plant or animal matter, the food is ground up inside its *pharynx* (throat). The resulting mash is further broken down inside the digestive tube, where nutrients are absorbed into the body. Undigested food and wastes exit through the anus.

The other roundworm innovation is blood cells. As we've seen, flatworms have no circulatory systems at all. Ribbon worms were the first to evolve blood vessels in which oxygen is carried throughout the body. In many roundworms, blood consists simply of a fluid in which molecules float. *Ascaris* has a different system, though. Hemoglobin, an oxygen-carrying molecule that's found in vertebrate red blood cells, carries oxygen inside the worm's blood vessels. Scientists suspect that *Ascaris* worms have hemoglobin to *remove* oxygen from their bodies—for them, oxygen is deadly.

Roundworms are covered in a cuticle, which protects their bodies in harsh environments. As the worm grows, its skin becomes too tight. Like snakes, roundworms can simply shed their skins and replace them. Although the cuticle provides good protection, it's not very flexible. As a result, roundworms tend to whip wildly from side to side when swimming, instead of gliding along smoothly.

Of all the world's roundworms, about thirty-six species are human parasites. Even ancient Egyptians were familiar with the large *Ascaris* worms, which live in human intestines. A 3,500-year-old scroll found in a tomb describes methods used to treat *Ascaris* infections. Roundworms are usually quite small or even microscopic, but the species that parasitize sperm whales may reach 43 feet (13 meters) in length. Other roundworms are plant parasites that can cause significant damage to farm crops. Each worm specializes on a particular type of plant and usually attacks the root systems.

Yet while some roundworms are pests, others are actually beneficial to us. Many species are *decomposers*, which eat dead and decaying materials that would otherwise pile up like uncollected garbage. Other roundworms are predators that filter through soils, hunting bacteria and microscopic organisms. Some parasitic species infect insects, such as fleas, weevils, and rootworms, which normally destroy farm crops. In fact, researchers are experimenting with five roundworm species, applying them to agricultural crops in an effort to control more damaging pests and avoid using chemical pesticides. Gardeners use roundworms, too, to combat beetle larvae that might otherwise wipe out a whole garden in no time.

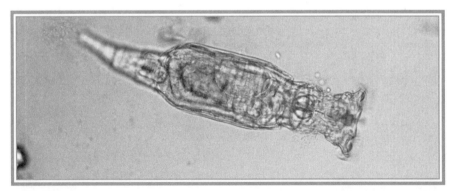

Rotifers are smaller than many single-celled creatures, measuring less than 0.02 inches (0.5 millimeter) from "crown" to "foot."

Survivors

Nematodes reproduce at an astonishing rate. Unlike flatworms that possess both sets of sex organs, individual nematode worms are either male or female. A female roundworm may store millions of eggs inside her body and can lay 200,000 eggs or more in a single day. The tiny eggs are so light that they can be picked up by wind and blown far and wide.

With so many eggs going out into the world each day, it seems as though the planet should be overrun by roundworms. But the eggs are an important food source for other animals and rarely survive to adulthood. Once roundworms hatch, larvae and adults have some amazing survival mechanisms. When the climate is harsh, roundworms can become dormant, halting all of their bodily functions until conditions improve.

The life cycle of such "helpful" roundworms is remarkably complex, involving four larval stages in addition to the adult worm. Almost all of these stages require an insect host as well as soil and water for the worms to travel through. It's the third larval stage that interests gardeners and researchers. It is at this point that the roundworm kills its insect host. Working together, a group of microscopic roundworm larvae can eat even a large insect's body in two weeks. Once the food is gone, roundworms "abandon ship" all at once, heading off in search of another meal.

THE ROYAL ROTIFERS

Sitting atop the "head" end of one of Earth's smallest animals is a whirling crown of cilia. Members of the phylum Rotifera are named for this unusual feature: *rota* is Latin for "wheel." At less than 1/50th of an inch (0.05 centimeter) in length, rotifers are smaller than many single-celled creatures. Yet rotifers are multicellular animals with bodies made up of hundreds of cells.

Although rotifers live everywhere—in puddles and soil, on the mosses that blanket tree trunks, in the frozen Arctic, and even in rain gutters on roofs—most of us will never see them unless we use a microscope. If you don't have a microscope handy, imagine a wine glass minus its flattened base. This is almost the exact shape of a rotifer. The narrow "stem" is actually a foot, complete with one or two tiny toes. When the rotifer finds a choice spot for feeding, it may glue itself in place for a while by emitting a sticky substance from its toe.

The "cup" portion of a rotifer's body is filled with reproductive and digestive organs. The crown of cilia, atop the "rim" of the cup, waves rapidly back and forth. This movement creates a current that draws in food, like water being sucked down a bathtub drain. Rotifers have light–sensitive eyespots, helping them find their

A Newly Discovered Animal

Symbion pandora, a tiny, barrel-shaped creature discovered in a Swedish harbor in 1995, makes its home in a most unusual place: on the bristly lips of a lobster.

Symbion is quite different from other animals. It's so unusual, in fact, that scientists created a new phylum for it, Cycliophora. This animal, just over 1/100 of an inch (0.03 centimeters) long, has an odd series of larval stages—some are free-swimming and others remain fastened in one spot,

while some feed and some don't. Its reproductive cycle is weird too. During the feeding stage, *Symbion* attaches itself to a lobster's bristles using a sucker on its foot. During this time, the animal reproduces asexually by budding. When the host lobster grows so big that it needs to *molt* (shed its skin), *Symbion* begins to reproduce sexually. The larvae let go and float off, not feeding until they find another lobster host.

way. They also have paired jaws, which they use to grind food before it enters their stomachs, and thick skins.

Now and then, rotifer colonies occur. A colony is made up of dozens of individual rotifers attached to one another in a circle by their sticky toes. The colony spins in the water as it moves along in search of food. The colony can tackle larger prey and protect itself better than can single rotifers.

Rotifers, like many of the tiny creatures that live in soil and water, play a vital role in our world as decomposers. Some rotifer species are so well suited to eating trash that they live in sewage-treatment tanks.

When it comes to reproduction, rotifers take several approaches. Most species have no males and reproduce using a method called *parthenogenesis*. This is actually a method of cloning in which females lay eggs that develop without being fertilized. Parthenogenesis among some rotifers produces only female offspring. Other rotifers produce male and female eggs. Males produced in this way, however, are small and survive long enough only to produce sperm and to mate. Like nematodes, rotifer eggs can go into a dormant state during a drought, coming "back to life" when water becomes available again.

CHAPTER SIX

M O L L U S K S

Imagine Earth 550 million years ago. No living thing had yet made its way onto land, but the oceans swarmed with bacteria, single-celled and multicellular plankton, sponges, and cnidarians.

A new kind of animal was beginning to show up, as well, crawling along the ocean floor. Unlike the loose-bodied animals that had come before it, this creature had a hard shell. This hard-bodied invertebrate and others like it would soon live in oceans and even make it onto land, becoming one of the most diverse animal groups on the planet—the mollusks.

SHELLED NEIGHBORS

The chances are that you've never seen a "wild" sponge, cnidarian, flatworm, or roundworm. But you probably pass by (or step over) a member of the phylum Mollusca almost every day. Snails and slugs can be found right in your own backyard or schoolyard. Winding, silvery trails reveal their nighttime journeys among plants and fallen leaves. Other familiar mollusks include clams, oysters, sea slugs, octopuses, and squids.

Mollusks can live in water that's salty or fresh, shallow or deep, warm or cold. They're found in almost every habitat on land too—from rain forests to deserts and from mountaintops to city dumps. Some have even permanently lost their shells. If you scooped up a bucket of seawater, you might find a full-grown pill clam only 0.25 inches (6 millimeters) long, or an octopus measuring 0.4 inch (one centimeter) from head to tentacle-tip. Then again, giant clams grow up to 4 feet (1.25 meters) in width, and giant squids can reach lengths of 60 feet (18 meters).

MOLLUSK BODIES

Mollusk means "soft," although that's hardly an unusual quality among the invertebrates we've studied so far. What set the first

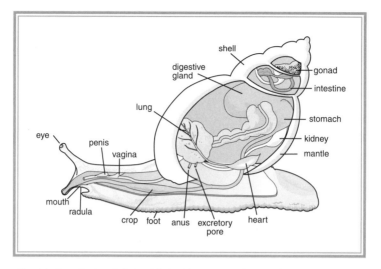

A mollusk's body is divided into three main regions: foot and head, body cavity (containing gills and other organs), and mantle.

mollusks apart was the "package" in which those soft bodies were wrapped: the shell. The rest of the body can be divided into three main regions: the foot and head, the body cavity, and the *mantle*. Snails provide a good example of the "typical" mollusk.

A snail, crawling along on its belly with a shell perched on its back, resembles a tiny, legless turtle. Despite all appearances, its wide, fleshy "belly" is actually a foot. A layer of mucus creates a slippery surface on which the foot can glide. This fluid also keeps land snails cool and moist and tastes bad to most predators. The snail's head extends off one end of its foot, perched on a long, flexible neck. Sets of tentacles that extend off the head are sensitive to light, odors, and touch.

Dozens of rows of tiny teeth cover the snail's muscular tongue, called the *radula*. When rubbed against an algae-covered rock or other surface, the radula works like sandpaper to grind off bits and pieces of food. A mollusk may have 250,000 teeth on its radula. When the teeth become worn from constant use, new ones grow in.

All of the snail's internal organs for digestion, excretion, circulation, and reproduction are sandwiched between its shell and its foot. Another cavity can be found under the back edge of the

Ever-Changing Oysters

Oysters take an interesting approach to life: they start out as males and finish as females.

When the water along their shoreline homes begins to warm in late spring, young male oysters are prompted to release sperm just as females begin to release eggs. Fertilized eggs float in the water for less than a day before hatching into microscopic larvae. Each larva is round, with a band of cilia around its middle. The cilia beat in the water, filtering food and moving the tiny larvae along. Just a day later, the larvae metamorphose. The oyster's second larval stage has a paper-thin shell, a foot, and more cilia than the first.

The next two weeks are a vulnerable time in the life of a little oyster. Although each female oyster may produce a million eggs, on average only one of that million will live. Most become food for larger animals. Any lucky survivors settle to the seabed and latch onto solid surfaces like rocks, the shells of other oysters, or sometimes boxes left behind by oyster farmers. After a year or two, males turn into females. And females they'll remain for the rest of their lives.

shell, which contains the *gills*. Gills, which evolved in mollusks before they did in other animals, contain masses of spongy, blood-filled tissue arranged in fine strands like the teeth on a comb. Each gill segment is lined with cilia, which beat constantly to draw water into the mantle cavity. Oxygen from the water flows through the gill tissue and is absorbed into the blood, which carries it throughout the body. At the same time, carbon dioxide (a toxic waste product) is removed from the blood through the gills.

A sheet of skin called the mantle covers the organs and foot. The mantle secretes mucus that contains a mix of proteins and calcium carbonate—the same chalky material found in some sponge spicules and in the shells of reef corals—which hardens to form the shell. Mollusks never grow out of their shells. Instead, the mantle slowly adds material to the shell's edges, increasing its size to accommodate the animal's growth.

The variety of mollusks we see around us today are all based on this same body plan. Scientists use the shell, the foot, the nervous system, and even the arrangement of teeth on a mollusk's radula to organize species into seven distinctive classes.

CHITONS

The taxonomic name given to chitons is Polyplacophora, which means "carrying many plates." These "plates" are actually segments of shell, seven or eight of which overlap along the animal's back. These shells provide excellent protection but are also flexible, allowing a chiton to mold itself to whatever rough surface it crawls over or to curl up into a tight ball to protect its delicate underside. Chitons are common residents of tide pools and shorelines, although they're so well camouflaged—in shades of brown, orange, green, or black—that many people (and predators) pass them right by.

A chiton's foot wields an incredible amount of suction power—to pry one off its chosen rock-home, you may have to use a knife. Over the course of time, each chiton sculpts a shallow indentation in the rock in the exact shape of its body. It will leave only at night, moving a short distance to feed on seaweed, algae, or small mussels.

TUSK SHELLS

It's easy to see where tusk shells got their name—they're long and curved, just like miniature elephant tusks. Tusk shells live buried head first in the sand and have been found in water 14,990 feet (4,570 meters) deep.

The shell of this mollusk is round and hollow, and its head is shovel-shaped for burrowing. Thin tentacles reach off the head,

The Oddball Mollusks

Scientists have been familiar with deep-sea limpets for a long time as fossils. These members of the class Monoplacophora, with their 1-inch (2.5-centimeter), cone-shaped shells, were thought to have gone extinct over 250 million years ago.

In the 1950s, members of a scientific expedition working off Mexico's Pacific Coast brought up a sample of mud from the ocean bottom 11,800 feet (3,600 meters) down. Among the animals in the sample, live deep-sea limpets were found. About a dozen species have now been identified in other parts of the world. Apparently, deep-sea limpets have survived the ages hidden away in deep ocean environments that we've only recently had the technology to explore.

Although their shells and muscular feet identify them as mollusks, monoplacophores are quite different in some important ways. Some of their internal organs occur in series, each in a different segment of the body. This kind of *segmentation* is common in earthworms and their relatives, but unheard-of among other mollusks.

Even stranger than the deep-sea-limpets are the aplacophores. Although these small animals look like worms and have no shells, they do have radulas and mantles. Instead of producing a shell, the mantle is loaded with spicules for protection, like those of the sponges. Aplacophores are usually found in water more than 9,840 feet (3,000 meters) deep, where they live among sand grains and mud and feed on small cnidarians.

feeling for single–celled organisms in the sand. A few interesting traits set tusk shells apart from other mollusks. Tusk shells have no gills, but instead use their mantles to absorb oxygen. To aid in this, the "tail" end of the shell is open and sticks up out of the sand, letting water flow into the shell from above. Unlike many other mollusks, tusk shells are either male or female throughout their lives, and the females produce only one egg at a time.

SNAILS AND SLUGS

Snails and slugs make up the phylum Gastropoda. They're the only mollusks found on land, as well as the most common mollusks in saltwater and freshwater habitats.

Gastropods are extremely flexible in their choices of food. On land, plant-eating snails and slugs are considered pests, almost always eating the "good" plants while ignoring weeds. But they often eat dying plants, providing an important scavenging service. Some gastropods are hunters. The oyster drill, whelk, and conch snail (all found in the ocean) are particularly fierce. These use their radulas as drills to pierce oyster shells and scrape out the meat. Other snails, like the augers and cones, have poison-barbed radulas to sting their prey.

In the ocean, snails and slugs breathe using gills. Fingerlike tufts of gills are scattered all over the bodies of nudibranchs, the lovely sea slugs. Land-living gastropods have *lungs* instead of gills. Lungs are air pockets inside an animal's body. The lining of these pockets is always moist and easily absorbs oxygen. Take a close look at a slug and you'll notice a small hole on the right side of its body, behind its head. This hole constantly opens and closes, pumping air into the snail's lungs. Freshwater snails also have lungs and must come out of the water to breathe.

Many gastropods, especially those living on land, are camouflaged in plain colors that match the soil and fallen leaves among which they crawl. If you want color, however, look no farther than the beautiful nudibranchs. *Chromodoris boucheti*, for example, has an iridescent blue mantle with a black "bull's-eye" pattern, and orange tentacles and gills. *Phyllidia polkadotsa* is lemon-yellow with black polka dots. Such coloration is a warning to potential predators—many nudibranchs are poisonous.

Natural works of art, gastropod shells come in a remarkable variety of shapes and colors. Shell exteriors may be as smooth as glass or marked with ridges, knobs, and sharp spines. Some are coiled and twisted like a turban or a carpenter's screw. Rainbows or a milky sheen mark the undersides of many shells. Leopard spots, zebra stripes, candy-cane swirls—no look is too gaudy or too elegant for the gastropods.

BIVALVES

Bivalves are a favorite food of people around the world. The name describes their paired shells, or valves, which are hinged together like the top and bottom halves of a treasure chest.

Their closed-in lifestyle requires bivalves to stay put most of the time, and their soft bodies have adjusted accordingly. Bivalves have no recognizable head. To breathe and eat, they simply open their shells. The gills filter out food particles as well as oxygen. Clams and other burrowing species take a slightly different approach—a pair of tubelike siphons extends off their mantles, reaching into the water like snorkels. One siphon pulls water in, while the other pushes out filtered water and wastes. When not feeding, bivalves clap their shells shut. Powerful muscles at the hinge hold the two

Scallops are bivalves with up to two hundred
light-sensitive eyes lining their shells.

shell-halves together, creating a watertight seal. Bivalves are safe this way even when exposed to air, and predators must work hard to break in.

Some bivalve shells look like bowls or spoons. Others take on more elaborate shapes, like fans, hammers, teardrops, knife blades, or hearts. Shells may be flat or fat and can be white, clear, or brightly colored. The differences are usually determined by lifestyle. Razor clams and other deep-burrowing bivalves have long, narrow shells that slide easily through the sand. Scallops, by contrast, "swim" by snapping their fan-shaped shells open and closed. Their narrow shells cut smoothly through the water, allowing them to make "leaps" of up to 20 inches (51 centimeters) when they're alarmed.

While bivalves aren't "smart" in the way that humans are, they're well prepared for their way of life. Giant clams are sensitive to light, closing their shells when the shadow of a potential predator passes over. Scallops, those most mobile of bivalves, watch for danger using rows of eyes along the edges of their shells. A scallop can have as many as two hundred pinpoint-size eyes, which are sensitive to changes in light. A razor clam reacts to danger by shooting water out the edges of its shells while pushing hard with its muscular foot, diving deeper into the sand.

THE SWIMMING MOLLUSKS

Octopuses, squids, and cuttlefishes are visibly different from other mollusks. They have no external skeletons, and instead of crawling or sitting on the ocean floor, they are strong swimmers. Nautiluses are swimmers, too, but grow swirling, chambered shells and live inside them.

Although cephalopods look different from other mollusks, they're actually built on the same basic plan—there's a foot-head region, a mantle, and a shell. The foot has been divided into a number of long, flexible tentacles that work for swimming, "walking" on the seafloor, collecting food, touching, and tasting.

Cephalopods, like this Pacific giant octopus, are shell-less mollusks. Millions of color cells under the octopus's skin allow it to blend in with its environment or show emotions.

Males even use one of their tentacles to pass sperm into a female's body. While octopuses, squids, and cuttlefishes have eight or ten tentacles, a nautilus may have as many as ninety.

The large, balloon-shaped sac above the tentacles looks like a head, but isn't—it's the mantle, which contains the cephalopod's organs. The head sits just above the tentacles, where they join the mantle.

While nautiluses are the only cephalopods with shells surrounding their bodies, a flat piece of shell is hidden inside the mantles of squids and cuttlefishes. Among all the mollusks, only the octopus has no trace of a shell whatsoever.

A cephalopod's eyes are one of its most astounding features. They're large and very similar in structure to the eyes of vertebrate animals. Unlike other mollusks, or any invertebrates before them, cephalopods can determine the shapes of objects. Their large eyes are also sensitive to the smallest changes in light and shading. Because the eyes are located on opposite sides of the head, many cephalopods can see in a full circle around them. The vampire squid, a resident of deep, dark seas, has larger eyes in proportion to its body size than any other animal on Earth—they're 1 inch (2.54 centimeters) across, while the squid itself is only 6 inches (15 centimeters) long. Cephalopods have large brains, too, and show an obvious curiosity about the world around them.

Cephalopods swim as though backstroking, moving eyes-up and mantle-first through the water. They may drift with the currents or use their tentacles to swim slowly. When a cephalopod wants to move fast, as when fleeing a predator, it uses jet propulsion. Siphons on either side of the head are generally used for breathing, but when threatened, a cephalopod can shoot water rapidly from them. This sends the animal speeding backward through the water. These jets of water are sometimes so forceful that they rocket the animal right out of the water.

The boneless, shell-less bodies of octopuses are so flexible that even large species can squeeze into narrow rock crevices. Some of the smaller octopuses have even discovered that aluminum cans tossed overboard from boats make great "caves." When they can't escape or hide from predators, however, octopuses and other cephalopods have a number of good defenses. Many produce a kind of ink, which they spit out in a cloud to confuse predators. Others are able to change colors rapidly in order to camouflage themselves among their surroundings. Under an octopus's skin lie countless color cells in a rainbow of shades, each of which is controlled by nerves. The octopus can contract or enlarge these cells in seconds, creating a variety of color patterns that flash across its skin. Such rapid color changes also work to show the octopus's mood—white when it's afraid, orange when it's ready to mate, red or purple when it's angry.

TASTY!

Head to a grocery store or drop by a restaurant and you'll soon discover what people like best about mollusks: their flavor. Calamari, oysters on the half-shell, and escargot are all delicious, but the next time you take a spoonful of clam chowder or some other mollusk meal, give a moment's thought to all the evolutionary innovations that went into producing that tasty morsel.

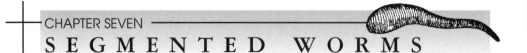

CHAPTER SEVEN

SEGMENTED WORMS

While many worms look alike, they're actually as diverse in appearance and lifestyle as any other animals in the world. Worms are also innovators. Remember, they were the pioneers of bilateral symmetry, the one-way digestive system, and the circulatory system. Worms were also the first animals to have heads and tails. The phylum Annelida takes these "creepy crawlers" in a new direction, where bodies are divided into segments.

ANNELIDS, INSIDE AND OUT

From the outside, annelids seem much like other worms—long, thin, and wiggly. There are some similarities on the inside too. Like other worms, the annelid's body plan is "a tube within a tube." The "inside tube" is the long, hollow intestinal tract. The "outside tube," called the *coelom*, surrounds the intestine like a long-sleeved shirt covers your arm. All the organs are enclosed in the spaces between the "sleeve" and the "arm."

Another special annelid characteristic is immediately visible: except for its head and tail, an annelid's body is divided into a series of ringlike segments. These rings are created by walls of muscle that separate the coelom into compartments. Each segment surrounds part of the digestive tract and also contains its own set of organs—nerve bundles, waste-removal organs, and blood vessels for circulation.

LEECHES, BRISTLEWORMS, AND EARTHWORMS

For 500 million years, segmented worms have wriggled through Earth's seas, soils, and sands. Today, about 13,500 annelid species have been named, and more are discovered every year. They're divided into three classes: bristleworms, earthworms, and leeches.

Dive into the ocean to find the bristleworms. Bristleworms are the most ancient and diverse annelids. Bundles of furry or feathery

Bristleworms, relatives of earthworms and leeches, have
iridescent bristles that reflect light in a rainbow of colors.

bristles dangle from each of their segments, making these worms look like swimming caterpillars or living feather dusters. Rows of fleshy "oars," called *parapodia*, line bristleworms' bodies and are used for swimming. Tentacles help bristleworms sense their environments and, in a few cases, are used to capture food.

An earthworm is like a long, flexible straw that is pointed at each end. The worm's head and tail are hard to tell apart, but it helps to locate the *clitellum*. This reproductive organ, which looks like a wide, pale-colored belt around the worm's body, is located closer to the head. Earthworms grow quite long, adding segments throughout their lives. The giant earthworms of Australia are the largest, stretching to 11 feet (3.4 meters) and containing hundreds of segments.

Leeches live in freshwater, oceans, and soil. One Asian species even thrives at altitudes up to 11,000 feet (3,354 meters) in the Himalaya Mountains. Leeches are different from other annelids in some interesting ways. Their body segments don't extend all the way from the skin to the intestinal tract, allowing for a more open coelom. Leeches also tend to be bristle-free. Because they can grow only a maximum of thirty-four segments, leeches are rarely more than 12 inches (30 centimeters) long. Their shape is different too.

Leeches have leaf-shaped bodies—flattened from top to bottom, with a wide middle and tapered ends.

Although we often think of worms as being plain-looking, many annelids are actually bright and colorful. Swimming bristleworms shimmer with iridescent red, green, or blue. Tubeworms are often blood red. Some earthworms have *bioluminescence*—they radiate light. At least one Australian earthworm species secretes a chemical in its skin mucus that is left behind as a glowing green trail. Bristleworms in the genus *Eunice* are bioluminescent when mating, using light to attract members of the opposite sex.

A CLOSER LOOK

The annelid body plan is wonderfully well organized. At the head is a mouth. Food passes though a muscular "chewing" organ, the pharynx. Beyond the pharynx lies a *crop*, a pocket where food is stored. The *gizzard* is a stomachlike organ that grinds food into a soft mash. Ground food enters the long, hoselike intestine, where nutrients are absorbed. Wastes pass out the far end of the worm's body through the anus. Alongside the pharynx in the head are a number of other vital organs. The worm's brain is located there, and its blood vessels begin there as well.

Annelids collect oxygen by using the same method as many other invertebrates: they absorb it through their skins. This requires water, of course, or at least moisture. Earthworms and leeches secrete a slimy substance onto their skins that helps them stay moist, but they must still live in damp environments. This explains why earthworms come out only during the cool nighttime hours or when rain floods them out of their burrows.

Annelids that live in water don't have to worry about drying out, but a few bristleworms (the elegant fanworms, for example) improve their oxygen-collecting ability by using gills. To get oxygen to every part of the body, annelids have a ladder-shaped network of blood vessels. There's no muscular heart to pump this blood, however. Instead, muscles squeeze the vessels open and closed, forcing the blood to move forward. Long vessels run down each side of the annelid's body, with smaller vessels reaching into each segment.

Don't be fooled by the simple appearance of annelids. A two-part brain sits in the worm's head, connected to a nerve cord that extends down its back. This nerve cord has extensions into each segment, making the worm highly sensitive to touch. Annelids have sense organs for touch and smell, and can detect light. A few species even have true eyes, with lenses capable of seeing images.

MOVE IT!

Because their bodies are broken into small units, each of which contains many muscles, segmented worms have a great deal of strength and control over their movement.

For earthworms, movement is a segment-by-segment activity. When the muscles of a particular segment contract, the segment folds up like an accordion. Bristles on other segments dig into the surface, providing traction. In the meantime, the worm braces its tail against the ground and gives a push. This creates a wavelike motion that travels through the worm's body. A thin mucus (secreted by the worm's skin to help it stay moist) gives the worm a slick surface on which to move.

Ocean-dwelling bristleworms have parapodia, which they use like oars. Right and left parapodia are moved separately, creating a graceful side-to-side swimming motion. Not all bristleworms are swimmers, though. Many—the lugworms and lovely feather-duster worms, for example—stay in one place, burrowed into the sand or inside their own hard tubes. Usually, a bristleworm builds its tube by secreting mucus from its skin and then stirring up sand and other materials from the surrounding seafloor. These particles

Dr. Leech

Unlike many of the flatworms and roundworms, parasitic leeches don't live on (or in) their hosts. Instead, they make their homes in warm, damp soil or water, attaching themselves to the bodies of other animals only long enough to feed.

Leeches are perfectly suited to their way of life—so well suited, in fact, that hosts often have no idea the leeches are there. After slicing through a host's skin with razor-sharp jaws or using chemicals to digest through the skin, a leech deposits a numbing anesthetic so its "blood donor" feels no pain. An important part of the leech's feeding system involves a chemical called *hirudin*, which prevents blood from clotting and helps the worm feed quickly. One good meal—less than half an ounce (15 milliliters) of blood—can satisfy a leech's hunger for six months.

Strange as it may seem, leeches have been used in medicine for thousands of years. Leeches were placed on a patient's body and allowed to remove "bad blood." It's been a long time since "leeching" was an acceptable form of treatment, but today leeches are being recognized for other medical benefits. Some doctors apply leeches to injuries (like black eyes) in which blood gathers under the skin. Researchers are also experimenting with hirudin, which may be useful as an anesthetic, to dilate blood vessels and to reduce swelling.

stick to the mucus, and the whole mixture hardens into a worm-shaped shell.

Leeches, which have no bristles and only partially segmented bodies, use their suckers to move. One sucker is found at each pointed end of the leech's body. When resting or waiting for prey to come by, a leech typically hangs on to a solid surface, using the sucker at its head. Wonderfully agile, leeches are able to hold their bodies upright, feeling for movement in the air or water around them. Special organs on the leech's skin are sensitive to light, heat, and smell. Some species even have simple eyes.

WORM FOOD

Annelids have widely varied appetites. Swimming bristleworms, for example, are predators with sharp jaws. Held inside the mouth most of the time, the jaws are pushed out when it's time to take a bite. Earthworms also hunt small invertebrate prey or sift through water and soil for food particles.

The tube-dwelling bristleworms tend to be filter-feeders, remaining hidden in their hard shells with only their heads sticking out to feed. Feather-duster worms are tubeworms named for their colorful crown of tentacles, which fan the water to draw in bits and pieces of food. Other bristleworms, like the Pompeii worms that live on the floor of the Pacific Ocean, collect bits of dead plant and animal matter that drift down to the bottom.

It wasn't long ago that earthworms were considered pests. Worms were held responsible for everything from crop damage to insanity and illness. Fortunately, over the past few centuries, people have figured out that earthworms are quite beneficial to humans. Farmers would be in big trouble without them, as would rain forests and other places where wild plants grow in abundance.

Earthworms feed by pushing their upper bodies out of the soil and feeling around for bits of plant litter. The worm uses its excellent sense of taste to choose pieces of food from its favorite plants. Back underground, the food is chewed and digested, and the wastes are passed into the soil. This process releases minerals from rotting plants back to the soil to be recycled by living plants.

As they burrow, worms loosen the soil, allowing rainwater and oxygen to enter more easily. They also move deep soil layers upward, keeping topsoil fresh. In a single acre of soil, earthworms may move as much as 100 tons (101,600 kilograms) of material per year.

Earthworms feed on decomposing plants, recycling nutrients back into the soil.

GO EAT A WORM!

Jellies, flatworms, sea stars, fishes, moles, skunks, and owls are but a few of the animals that eat annelids. With all those hungry mouths around, a little annelid would hardly seem to stand a chance.

Yet worms do have ways of protecting themselves. One approach is regeneration. When attacked, an earthworm hides its head and digs its bristles into the soil as anchors. A hungry fish or robin might be able to pull off its tail, but as long as the worm's head and at least thirty-four of its segments remain, it will regenerate its lost segments in a few weeks. Bristleworms can also replace lost parapodia.

Staying alive sometimes requires a good offense too. The fireworm, an Australian bristleworm, is well equipped for self-protection. If a predator comes near enough to touch the fireworm, its sharp bristles shatter and stick in the attacker's skin. The sensation is like stepping on glass and is sure to leave a lasting reminder: when you see a fireworm, swim the other way!

Scaleworms, better known as sea mice because of their furry, golden bristles, are another variety of bristleworm. In addition to bristles, sea mice are covered in hard, overlapping shields. When threatened, sea mice curl into balls, allowing their scales to protect them from hungry predators.

REGENERATION AND REPRODUCTION

Like flatworms, some annelids use regeneration as a means of a sexual reproduction. Freshwater annelids can divide their bodies along the middle, and each end will regrow its missing parts. Bristleworms sometimes reproduce asexually, too, growing buds that break off and can survive on their own.

Most annelids, however, undergo sexual reproduction. Every earthworm and leech has both male and female reproductive organs. Worm pairs line themselves up facing opposite directions, with their clitella—those pale bands near the head—touching. Each worm fertilizes the other's eggs. Within a day or two, earthworms begin to release their eggs in small groups, all enclosed in a jellylike fluid secreted by the clitellum. The fluid hardens into a cocoon, which slides off the worm's body and falls into the soil. It doesn't take long for the fertilized eggs to hatch. Young earthworms look like small copies of their parents and reach adulthood in a few months.

Unlike other annelids, bristleworms are either male or female. These marine worms go through a larval stage after hatching. Larvae float along in the water for a while and then metamorphose into their adult worm forms.

NOT QUITE ANNELIDS

A few other strange and unusual worms can be found in the oceans. They're different enough from annelids to be placed in their own phyla. One of these is the phylum Pogonophora.

Pogonophorans are tulip-shaped tube-dwellers that make their homes as much as 1.5 miles (2.4 kilometers) beneath the surface, living with their hind-ends buried in mud. They're not segmented like annelids, but otherwise they look and live much

Creatures of the Deep

In 1977 the crew of the submersible *Alvin* began exploring volcanoes that erupt on the deep seafloor. Called chimneys or smokers, these small volcanoes pour hot water and toxic hydrogen sulfide gases into the water. While the deep ocean is normally quite cold—only about 43 degrees Fahrenheit (6 degrees Celsius)—chimneys heat the surrounding water up to 176 degrees Fahrenheit (80 degrees Celsius), which is near the boiling point.

The *Alvin* researchers were delighted to find that each of these hot spots is like an oasis in the desert, squirming with life. Worms taller than an average human wave in the water, while crabs, clams, and shrimp set up house on the rocks surrounding chimney openings.

Pogonophorans are among the most common animals around these vents. They have no digestive organs or mouths. Instead, symbiotic bacteria live inside the worms' bodies. The worms use their tentacles to collect hydrogen sulfide and oxygen, on which bacteria feed from the water. In return, the bacteria produce molecules pogonophorans can use as food.

Annelid tubeworms take a different approach to feeding. They use their gills to filter chemicals from the water that have already been broken down by free-living bacteria. Not only do tubeworms thrive in the heat and darkness, but they may live as long as 250 years.

The *Alvin.*

like tubeworms. *Pogonophoros* is Greek for "beard-wearer," a description of the tentacles surrounding the worm's head and mouth.

WORMS, WORMS, EVERYWHERE

Segmented worms may be slimy and generally small, but even the least attractive among them play important roles in Earth's natural systems. Annelids recycle dead plants and animals on land and in the seas and keep soils fresh and healthy. Some annelids consume insect pests. Worms are important food sources for countless larger animals, and leeches are used in human medicine. They are, as the Greek philosopher Aristotle once said, "Earth's guts"—the living heart of our planet.

CHAPTER EIGHT

ARMORED ANIMALS, PART ONE: CHELICERATES, CRUSTACEANS, AND MYRIAPODS

HISTORY IN THE ROCKS

In the Rocky Mountains of western Canada, you'll find a group of rocks that can take you back in time to the bottom of the sea 545 million years ago. Called the Burgess Shale, this rock formation is famous among biologists and *paleontologists* (scientists who study ancient life) because it contains a huge number of fossilized animals. About 150 species in at least fifteen separate phyla have been unearthed since the shale was discovered in 1909.

Shale is a kind of rock that often forms near shorelines, where fine particles of dirt are carried out to sea by rivers and wind. The seafloor in such areas is soft and gooey and makes a great home for bottom-dwelling invertebrates. The Burgess Shale formed at the edge of an underwater canyon, where mudslides often swept sections of the seabed, and anything living in them, over the edge. As the mud slowly hardened at the bottom of the canyon, dead animals trapped within it were often perfectly preserved.

The Burgess Shale was formed over the course of 20 million years. During this time, which scientists call the Cambrian Period, animal life exploded in diversity. Before the Cambrian Period, there were just a handful of animal phyla—mostly sponges and jellies. By its end, however, nearly every phylum of animals living today had evolved. Many of them are represented in the Burgess Shale. It's the most complete record of ancient animal history ever found.

Included among the fossils of the Burgess Shale are the oldest-known animals with hard, jointed skeletons covering their soft bodies. These invertebrates, members of the phylum

Arthropoda, evolved in the sea but later became the first animals to move out of the water and onto land.

WHAT MAKES AN ARTHROPOD?

It's easy to pick out a number of characteristics that set arthropods apart from other invertebrates. One of the first things you'll notice when looking at a crab, an insect, or another arthropod is that its body is divided into large segments. Each section of the arthropod's body plays a different role and contains a specific set of organs. There's a head, a *thorax* (similar to your chest), and an abdomen. Usually, each segment has a number of *appendages*, or extensions, such as legs, fangs, antennae, and pincers. Scientists use the number and arrangement of these appendages to divide arthropods into groups, including chelicerates (spiders, sea spiders, and horseshoe crabs), crustaceans (crablike animals), myriapods (millipedes and centipedes), and insects.

All of the invertebrates we've studied so far have had hydrostatic skeletons—body fluids enclosed inside an "envelope" of skin against which muscles can press. In mollusks, a hydrostatic skeleton controls some movements, but other actions (such as opening and closing the shell) are controlled by muscles pulling on and pushing against the shells. Arthropods have quite a different kind of skeleton, called an *exoskeleton* (*exo* means "outside"). It's made of *chitin*, a material that hardens into firm but flexible plates. Each section of the arthropod's body is covered in separate plates, but they're hinged to provide flexibility.

Hinged spaces between an arthropod's body plates are called *joints*. Arthropod joints work in much the same way as yours do. Your knee, for example, is a joint between your upper and lower leg. Muscles connect the bone to the joint. They contract to bend the leg and relax to unbend it. In an arthropod, muscles are attached to the inside edges of neighboring plates. As a result, although they're encased in "suits of armor," arthropods can walk, run, swim, or even fly. Arthropods were the first animals to come onto land, thanks to their exoskeletons. The hard covering prevents water loss, allowing them to live far from water without drying out. The exoskeleton also provides arthropods with solid, strong bodies that can move against the force of *gravity*.

One limitation of the exoskeleton is that it's not alive. It can't grow with the animal. Now and then arthropods must molt, or shed their exoskeletons, and grow larger replacements.

CHELICERATES

A variety of appendages is one of the most obvious traits of the arthropods. Chelicerates are no exception. These arthropods get their name from the first pair of appendages on their heads: their fangs, or *chelicerae*.

HORSESHOE CRABS

Don't be fooled by the horseshoe crab's name—it's no crab at all. Horseshoe crabs are related to spiders and scorpions. Although these creatures were incredibly diverse and abundant about 300 million years ago, today there are only four species. Horseshoe crabs make their homes in shallow water along coastlines where, during the breeding season, you can find them gathered by the thousands, mating and laying their eggs in the sand.

The horseshoe crab gets its name from the shape of its shell, which looks like an upside-down U or (you guessed it) a horseshoe. The U-shaped part of its body is divided in two parts, a *cephalothorax* (combined head and thorax) at the curve of the U and an abdomen at its end. A long, sharp tail extends off the abdomen, like the handle on a hairbrush. You can tell the horseshoe crab from a real crab by looking atop the cephalothorax—crabs have antennae, while horseshoe crabs don't. Instead, they feel around with their chelicerae to find food, and

Horseshoe crabs are ancient chelicerates that are often seen on shorelines, emerging from the ocean in large numbers to lay their eggs.

collect odors using sensitive hairs on their legs. Two *compound eyes* (with many lenses) located atop the cephalothorax are sensitive to light.

Turn a horseshoe crab over to find its appendages. The chelicerae are at the top of the cephalothorax, surrounding the slit-shaped mouth. Below these are five pairs of legs for walking. Horseshoe crabs have no jaws. Instead, they swim over their meals and grind them back and forth between their legs. Then they inhale the pieces. Under the abdomen are the *book lungs*—paper-thin stacks of tissues that absorb oxygen.

ARACHNIDS

If you're "creeped out" by the thought of scorpions, spiders, ticks, and mites, you're not alone. Most people go out of their way to avoid these particular arthropods. Yet arachnids are some of the most fascinating and useful creatures you'll ever meet.

Arachnids are often mistaken for insects, but they're really quite different. Arachnids (like their cousins, the horseshoe crabs) have

Spiders spin silk to build elaborate webs, protect their eggs, and move from place to place.

two body segments—a cephalothorax and an abdomen—while insects have three. Four pairs of walking legs extend off the arachnid's cephalothorax. Insects have three body segments—head, thorax, and abdomen—and six legs attached to the thorax. On the arachnid's head you'll find chelicerae and *pedipalps*, special appendages for finding and capturing food, but no antennae. Book lungs are located under the abdomen, and some arachnids have small holes in their abdomens to collect extra air.

Spiders are awesome predators, built for their lives' work: catching and eating insects. Their chelicerae are hollow and connected to poison glands, and their pedipalps are located forward on the head, like little arms designed to grab and hold prey. With prey "in hand," the spider immediately bites and injects a dose of venom, which paralyzes or kills the insect prey. The venom also works like an acid, liquefying the prey's body tissues. Once the venom has done its work, the spider uses its hollow fangs to "drink" its softened meal. Despite their gruesome way of feeding, most spiders eat flies and help keep other insect populations under control and make good neighbors in general.

All spiders are equipped with a set of silk-spinning organs called *spinnerets* located beneath their abdomens, with which they produce material to line nests, protect eggs, and move from place to place. Young spiders often use strands of silk as "balloons," sometimes drifting hundreds of miles on air currents before settling down to adult life in a new home. More than half the world's 35,000 spider species also use silk nets, or webs, to catch and immobilize their prey.

Web Masters

Web-building spiders are true artists, producing a wide variety of web types. Silk emerges from the spinnerets as a liquid. When hit by air, the liquid solidifies into a string that can be drawn out, cut, or attached to surfaces. Spider silk is twice as strong as steel and more flexible than a rubber band.

Some webs are built to function like sheets that catch falling and flying insects. Trapdoor spiders weave doors for their burrows, hiding underneath until vibrations warn them of passing insects. Cast-web spiders construct nets to "throw" over passing prey.

Orb webs are probably the most familiar to you, built by beautifully colored garden spiders and others. Strung across open spaces, orb webs catch the light and look like shimmering quilts or targets made of circles inside circles. To build an orb web, the spider first attaches lines of silk between solid braces (like tree branches or the walls of your house) to form a frame. Next, it draws lines from the braces toward a center point, like the spokes of a bicycle wheel. Finally, the spider weaves sticky strands into a spiral of "catch lines" that connect the spokes. The spider usually awaits "visitors" by standing on one of the frame lines. As soon as it feels vibrations on the web, the spider rushes forward, bites its prey and injects venom, and wraps its meal in a silky cocoon.

Wolf spiders and tarantulas are active hunters that chase down their prey, while the stocky little jumping spiders can leap several times their own body length to grab insects. Fishing spiders wait quietly by the water's edge and then run lightly across the water's surface to catch tadpoles and tiny fish.

Camouflage coloration helps most spiders blend into their surroundings. Desert spiders may be sand-colored, while those that live on soil are often brown or gray. The crab spiders, which hang out on flowers as they await prey, blend in with the variety of flower they most commonly visit.

Scorpions evolved well before the other arachnids. They're long and thin, with large, pinching claws on their pedipalps. The abdomen is tipped with a venomous stinger, the scorpion's tool for killing prey and fending off enemies. Scorpions are residents of some of the hottest climates on Earth. They spend the day hidden beneath rocks or logs, in caves, or underground and come out to hunt in the relative cool of night. Despite their fierce reputation, scorpions are caring parents. The young crawl atop their mother's cephalothorax, remaining there in safety for as long as two weeks before heading off to face the world on their own.

Ticks and mites are the smallest arachnids—only a few mite species grow longer than 0.04 inch (1 millimeter), and ticks are rarely more than 1.2 inches (3 centimeters) long. Most are parasites that live on plants and animals both on land and in water.

CRUSTACEANS

About 40,000 species strong, crustaceans are among the most common residents of seashores and oceans—and among the tastiest! Crabs, lobsters, and shrimp are crustaceans, as are less familiar animals such as barnacles, water and sand fleas, copepods, and pill bugs.

A crustacean usually has a single, hard plate made of chitin covering its head and thorax. Atop its head are one or more pairs of eyes (sometimes propped up on movable stalks) and four antennae. Larger crustaceans, such as lobsters, usually have long abdomens. Each of the three main body regions has its own appendages: jaws on the head, five or more pairs of walking legs on the thorax, and swimming legs on the abdomen. The appendages are often forked into two parts, as if the crustacean is flashing a peace sign. The two sections may have different functions— for example, a walking leg may have featherlike gills on its outside branch.

Crustaceans come in an impressive range of sizes. Giant spider crabs have been recorded with 12–foot (3.7–meter) leg spans and bodies 15 inches (38 centimeters) across. An American lobster may weigh 44 pounds (20 kilograms)—about as much as a four–year–old child. At the opposite extreme, water fleas are often no more than 1/1,000 of an inch (0.25 millimeters) long.

Fairy shrimp are among the most common crustaceans. These small, almost transparent animals live in both freshwater and

Like other crustaceans, lobsters have armorlike shells that protect their bodies and provide support for movement.

salt water and are an important food source for larger animals in both environments. The water flea, *Daphnia*, which you may have seen under a microscope in biology class, is a tiny, freshwater shrimp. Aquarium owners often buy live brine shrimp, another kind of fairy shrimp, to feed to their pet fishes. In nature, brine shrimp are found in some of the saltiest environments imaginable, including the Great Salt Lake in Utah, where water may be seven times saltier than seawater. The Great Salt Lake and other salty spots, like San Francisco Bay in California, are visited by millions of migratory birds each year. The birds stop over just to fatten up on brine shrimp before continuing their journeys.

Barnacles are an unusual group of crustaceans because they build shells that are similar to those of mollusks. A barnacle's volcano-shaped shell is open at the narrow top, and the wide bottom is cemented to a hard surface—a rock, a ship hull, a pier, or even the body of a whale. The little crustacean's feathery feet stick out of the shell when it feeds, waving to bring in food.

Copepods and decapods are also tiny, shrimplike crustaceans. Copepods may crawl around on the seafloor, float in tide pools, or spend their entire lives out in the open ocean. A few even make their homes in freshwater mountain lakes that are as high as 16,400 feet (5,000 meters) above sea level. Amphipods, meanwhile, are usually found on beaches, scavenging rotting piles of seaweed that wash up along the shoreline. Talk a walk on the beach, especially at night, and you'll find these little beasties bounding around on the sand. Their hopping movements have earned amphipods the common names "sand flea" and "beach hopper."

The best-known crustaceans are the ten-legged decapods: shrimp, crabs, and lobsters. These have large, pincerlike front legs and come in a variety of shapes and sizes. Hermit crabs squeeze themselves inside abandoned mollusk shells, carrying these "mobile homes" around as protection. Larger crabs have egg-shaped, flattened, square, or shield-shaped shells. Crabs are famous for their odd way of walking—they scoot sideways rather than moving headfirst. Like lobsters, crabs and shrimp are favorite food items of people around the world.

While we're on the subject of pods (which means "foot"), here's another group to check out: the isopods, which you may have met as a child. They include wood lice and "roly-polys," also called pill bugs, that live in grassy lawns and under houses, curling into perfect little balls when bothered. Isopods are the only crustaceans that live their entire lives on land.

You might be surprised to learn that the largest animal ever to live on Earth, the blue whale, feeds on 1-inch (2.5-centimeter) long crustaceans. The blue whale's favorite food is a tiny shrimp, the krill, which gathers in huge swarms in the cold waters of the Antarctic region.

Millipedes and centipedes were the first arthropods to evolve on land, 400 million years ago.

MYRIAPODS

Around 400 million years ago, myriapods—better known as centipedes and millipedes—became the first arthropods to evolve on land. Remove a myriapod's legs and it looks a lot like an annelid, with a long, tough-skinned body ringed by many segments. In a myriapod, however, these segments are simply separate plates of chitin that don't divide the animal internally. Dozens of short walking legs help myriapods burrow into the soil, scrabble through fallen leaves, or slide into tiny crevices among rocks, under tree bark, and in wood piles.

Millipedes are important members of forest communities, especially in the tropical rain forests, where they often turn over more soil each year than do earthworms. The head is the first segment, followed by a two-segment thorax. All of the legs are located on the abdomen, and there are two pairs per segment.

Millipedes may look scary, reaching lengths of 11 inches (28 centimeters) and marching purposefully along on dizzying waves of legs. They're completely harmless, however, with no poison and no inclination to bite. If threatened, a millipede simply rolls into a spiral-shaped ball. A nasty-tasting chemical in its skin provides extra protection from hungry predators. The leggiest of all millipedes is *Illacme plenipes*, a California species that boasts 375 pairs of legs.

The second group of well-known myriapods is the centipedes. They look similar to millipedes, with abdomens divided into many segments. But unlike millipedes, centipedes are swift-moving and prepared for aggressive action. Each segment bears only one pair of legs, which are often long and flexible for running. As meat-eaters, centipedes have antennae to feel for prey and legs that are modified for grabbing. Sharp, poisonous fangs surround the mouth to impale and immobilize fat insect larvae, slugs, worms, and other arthropods. While the centipede's bite isn't likely to kill a human, it's a stinging reminder that centipedes are more fun to watch than to touch.

ONLY THE BEGINNING

Today, arthropods are the most common animals in every habitat on Earth. About a million species of crabs and lobsters, spiders and scorpions, millipedes and centipedes, insects, and others have been discovered so far. Experts believe that as many as thirty times that number of arthropod species may actually exist.

CHAPTER NINE

ARMORED ANIMALS, PART TWO: INSECTS

Arachnids, crustaceans, and myriapods are amazingly diverse, yet they make up only a fraction of the species in Phylum Arthropoda. There's still one more group of arthropods to consider: class Insecta. Almost a million kinds of insects have been identified so far, and several thousand new species are discovered every year. We've hardly begun to explore the tropical rain forests, for example, where a single rain forest tree may be home to more than 160 kinds of insects. No one knows how many insect species may actually exist.

RECOGNIZING INSECTS

Though you'd hardly guess it by looking at them, insects are all closely related—from South American owlet moths that measure 12 inches (30 centimeters) from wingtip to wingtip, to dainty fairyfly wasps no larger than specks of dust. Some insects look like armored vehicles, while you'd easily mistake others for leaves or twigs.

It can also be confusing to tell some insects apart from other arthropods. The first trick is to look for wings—insects are the only arthropods (and, in fact, the only invertebrates) that have them. Don't be fooled if the animal in question is wingless, though. It may still be an insect. Some insects are wingless as adults, and many insects are wingless as juveniles or larvae. To find out if you're looking at an insect, start counting body parts. Adult insects have three body segments, six jointed legs, and two antennae. No other arthropods have this arrangement.

On an adult insect's head you'll find jaws, fingerlike *palpi* for grabbing food, two antennae, and a pair of compound eyes. The thorax is the middle body section, bearing the legs and, usually, a pair or two of wings. There are no appendages on the insect's long abdomen, but sometimes a stinger projects from its tip. If the insect is female, there may also be a set of pointy reproductive organs called *ovipositors*.

Every segment of an insect's body is covered in a waterproof cuticle, or tough skin made of chitin. The individual chitin plates are most obvious on the abdomen, where they form eleven overlapping rings. Upon close inspection, it looks as though a line of tiny holes has been punched along either side of the cuticle. These are the *spiracles*, which open into a series of air tubes and balloon-shaped air storage sacs. Insects need a lot of oxygen to fuel their flight muscles, and these air sacs contain their reserve supplies.

Muscles attach to the interior of each chitin segment, branching out to power the legs, wings, and other body parts. Every insect has a tiny brain with a long nerve cord. The mouth leads into a digestive tube that has special pockets along its length for grinding, storing, and digesting food. The last major organ is the heart, which extends like a lumpy garden hose along the insect's back.

THE WING'S THE THING

The wings of birds and bats, the flying vertebrates, contain bony "frames." Insect wings are made differently—they're branches of the exoskeleton that are supported by hollow air tubes and are hinged to the sides of the body. Wings gave early insects more freedom than any of the more primitive animals that came before them had. With the advantage of flight, insects can flee from danger, seek out new areas when food is scarce or weather is bad, and cover great distances in search of food and mates. With the power to

Insect wings are branches off the exoskeleton, hinged to the sides of the body. Dragonflies are the most ancient group of flying insects.

move, insects quickly spread across land and freshwater habitats, even reaching remote islands and high mountain peaks.

The first insect fliers were dragonflies, extra-large versions of the colorful species that dance over water today. A dragonfly's narrow, paired wings stick out from its sides like the stiff wings of an airplane. The wings can beat up and down, but cannot be folded back against the body. But dragonflies don't seem to suffer from this lack of wing flexibility. They can fly backward and are real speedsters, often zipping along at more than 36 miles (58 kilometers) per hour.

For comparison, consider the wings of a beetle and a bee. Beetles have two pairs of wings, each pair with a different shape and function. The flight wings are thin and filmy, like sheets of tracing paper. When a beetle is resting or walking, the flight wings lay folded against its body, covered by the second pair of wings, or elytra. Elytra are thick and strong, working like shields to protect the beetle's back. The beetle lifts its elytra high when it takes off, creating lift and giving the flight wings plenty of room to move.

Bees also have two pairs of wings, but both are used for flying. The wings on either side of the body are interlocked and form a sort of lopsided heart-shape that catches air with great efficiency.

HANDY LEGS

The most ancient living insect species, silverfish and springtails, evolved from millipedes and centipedes around 400 million years ago and are still common today. Silverfish and springtails have never had wings. Instead, these little creatures use their legs and three–forked tails to scoot and hop along. One push of its tail can send a quarter-inch (6.4-millimeter) long springtail sailing 4 inches (10 centimeters) forward. Fleas and lice are also wingless insects.

Most insects, even those with wings, spend a lot of time walking. Long, jointed legs give insects flexibility and strength, and their clawed feet are perfect for climbing and grasping. Houseflies are even able to walk on slick, vertical surfaces or while upside down, thanks to their sticky footpads. Grasshoppers and their relatives—including crickets, katydids, and locusts—have strong, extra-long legs that make their owners more athletic than Olympic long-jumpers. In a single leap, a grasshopper can travel more than twenty times its body length.

Praying mantises and mole crickets provide interesting examples of the many odd ways in which insect legs are sometimes modified. Mantises use their front legs to grab and hold food, so the legs are lined with sharp spines that stab their prey. Mole crickets have thick, shovel-like forelegs that are used to push dirt out of the way as they burrow underground. And we can't forget the swimmers. Look down into the water of a clear, slow-moving stream or pond and you may see water boatmen bugs just under the surface. One pair of their long legs is flattened to serve as oars.

INSECTS IN DISGUISE

Camouflage is an insect's best defense. Many species are green, brown, or gray—or some combination of those three colors—to blend in with leaves and soil. Leaf insects and walkingsticks, distant relatives of the grasshoppers, take camouflage to the extreme. Every part of a stick insect's body is shaped to look like a twig or a crusty piece of bark. These long, lanky insects are active at night. Days are spent perched on bushes or tree branches, not moving for hours at a time. They blend in so well that most predators pass them right by. Leaf insects have front wings shaped exactly like leaves, complete with green veins. Some are bright green like fresh leaves, while others are brown and spotted, like dead leaves that are beginning to decay. Even the leaf insect's legs imitate leaves.

Peppered moths are also camouflage experts. Their wings are dusty white with specks of gray and black. This coloration

Two color phases can be found among peppered moths. White moths with black spots are well camouflaged with lichen-covered trees, while dark individuals blend in against lichen-free trees.

Lights, Music, and Perfume

Insects might not be romantic, but they have some flashy ways of attracting mates. Step outside on a warm summer evening and you're likely to hear the creaky, chirrupy sound of male insects singing to attract females. Cicadas produce their songs by vibrating drumlike membranes inside their abdomens. The resulting thumps are so loud that females hear them as far as a quarter-mile (400 meters) away and can feel the drumming vibrations in the air. Crickets and grasshoppers take a different approach to singing. A male creates his song by rubbing parts of his body, usually wings and legs, against each other like a violinist pulling a bow across his instrument's strings. Ears, located on the forelegs or other parts of the body, allow females to hear the songs of competing male "musicians."

Another common sight on warm nights is the flickering yellow-green light of fireflies, a kind of beetle. Males signal their readiness to mate using a kind of "Morse code" sequence that is recognized only by females of the same species. Females can't fly, but they invite the winged males to join them by flashing a signal in return.

Emperor moths and many other insects use sweet-smelling chemicals to attract mates. Usually it's the female who produces these chemicals, which float off in the wind. Male emperor moths can detect a female's scent using their feathery antennae, even if she's as far as 6.8 miles (11 kilometers) away.

perfectly matches the lichens that cover their favorite trees. At rest on a tree, the peppered moth looks like a lump of lichen-covered bark.

OTHER DEFENSES

Although many insects are camouflaged, others are brilliantly marked and easy to see. This might seem dangerous, as predators can easily spot such insects. Most of the time, however, colorful insects are giving their predators a warning: "I'm poisonous!" When a bird or other predator is stung while trying to eat a bee or gets sick after swallowing a toxic monarch butterfly, the bright colors are impressed on its memory. It will avoid similar insects forever after.

Chemical weapons are common among insects as well. Bombardier beetles, stinkbugs, and stick insects spray toxins at enemies, and some katydids squirt blood. Blister beetles secrete a burning, acidic chemical onto their skin, and some ants inject toxins when they bite.

EATING UTENSILS

One source of diversity among insects is the variety of food sources they can utilize. Insects eat leaves or other plant parts, sip nectar or blood, collect pollen, chew into wood, or eat meat. The mouthparts of each species are adapted to a particular style of feeding.

Leaf-chomping insects, such as grasshoppers and many ants, have scissorlike jaws used for slicing through tough leaves and stems. Weevils have sharp jaws, too, placed at the tips of their very long "noses." These little insects, sometimes called elephant beetles, use their stretched-out snouts to bore through bark in order to reach their food of choice, the wood beneath. The jaws of insect-eating insects, like most beetles, are pincers built for holding prey and cutting it into pieces. Mosquitoes, by contrast, have sharply pointed, strawlike mouthparts used to penetrate skin and suck up blood or (in male mosquitoes) to drink nectar. The housefly has an especially weird way of feeding—it vomits acids that liquefy its food. Then the fly uses its soft lower lip as a sponge to soak up the meal.

The evolution of flowering plants about 130 million years ago gave insects an entirely new food source: nectar and pollen. Butterflies and moths are nectar-feeders, as are bees and wasps. Part of the butterfly's jaw is modified into a long, curly tube that can reach nectar hidden deep inside a flower. Bees don't have nectar-collecting tubes, but instead lap up the sugary liquid. Bees also feed on pollen, which contains a flowering plant's sperm cells, and butterflies are often dusted by the tiny pollen grains when dipping their heads into flowers. When the insects fly away, some of the pollen falls onto the next flowers they visit. Without even knowing it, insects help their favorite plants to reproduce.

TIME FOR A CHANGE

Although there's no easy way to sum up the life cycles of insects, most fall into two basic categories: incomplete metamorphosis and complete metamorphosis.

The more ancient insect species undergo *incomplete metamorphosis*. The young, called nymphs, hatch from their eggs looking like

Bees, butterflies, and beetles are insects that undergo complete metamorphosis before reaching adulthood. Here you can see the caterpillar, chrysalis, and butterfly stages of the monarch butterfly.

small, wingless versions of their parents. Grasshoppers undergo this life cycle, as do dragonflies. Many nymphs are carnivores that live in water. Nymphs use gills to breathe underwater, but will lose these as they approach adulthood and move onto land. At about the same time they'll begin to grow wings.

Like other arthropods, young insects must shed and replace their skin as they grow. Some insects go through just a few molts before reaching adulthood, while others molt dozens of times. To molt, an insect puffs itself up with air. The pressure splits the exoskeleton, and the insect pulls itself free. A larger cuticle, which has been growing underneath, begins to harden in the air. An insect's transition into adulthood is marked by one final molt—adults will not molt again before they die.

Insects that undergo *complete metamorphosis* really do experience a complete change in shape and form. Bees, butterflies, and beetles are among the insects that have this type of life cycle. It all begins with a fertilized egg. Insects may leave their eggs inside pieces of fruit, under leaves, or atop piles of decomposing plants or meat, providing an immediate food source for their hatching young. Bees and wasps keep eggs inside their nests and bring food to their larvae.

When this kind of larva hatches, it looks nothing like its parents. In fact, the difference in appearance is so extreme that early biologists sometimes mistook larvae and adults of the same insects for entirely different species. Some larvae are agile carnivores or herbivores, with legs for walking around. Others are legless grubs. After the larva has completed its growth, it settles down in a safe spot and a thick case forms around its body. Inside, the larva literally melts away. Its cells then reorganize themselves into an entirely different shape. A wormlike, leaf-eating caterpillar, for example, becomes a delicate, winged butterfly.

LIVING TOGETHER

If you've ever seen a line of ants marching through the grass or watched a wasp nest grow under the eaves of your house, you've seen some examples of another interesting insect behavior: social living. Many insects—including ants, termites, bees, and wasps—gather in large groups, cooperating to divide the work of life. Individuals in a colony may even take on different shapes to help them perform their roles. Colonies vary in size, as well—large- bodied ant species might have only a few individuals in a nest, while termite colonies can include several million individuals.

Ant colonies typically contain workers, soldiers, and reproducers. The queen is the heart of the colony. She mates with winged males and lays all the colony's eggs. Wingless female worker ants wander outside in search of food. They mark their trails using chemicals that other workers can detect and follow. Inside the nest, workers may be responsible for caring for young, sorting food, or excavating new tunnels. Soldiers have extra-large jaws for biting and hover around the colony to chase off predators and invaders.

Colonial insects, such as wasps, bees, ants, and termites, live in large groups. Members of a colony may be workers, soldiers, or nannies or may live only to reproduce.

Bees and wasps also use class systems in their colonies, which include queens, drones (reproductive males), nannies, and workers. Their nests are made up of attached, apartment-like units that house food, eggs, and larvae. Workers communicate using complex dances, which describe where pollen and nectar can be found to other insects.

The social organization of a termite colony and its division of labor are similar to the social organization of ants and bees. There are a few reproductive colony members, including a massive queen who may live for fifty years, and lots of workers. On the plains of Australia and Africa, termite mounds can easily be mistaken for rock formations—they're large and complex, as hard as cement, and often as tall as a two-story building. Food is stored below ground, and the young remain safely tucked away in the "basement" of the nest. Termites are a favorite food of many birds and mammals, but the rock-hard nest is not easy to break into.

MAYBE THEY'RE NOT SO AWFUL

There's no doubt about it: insects can be pesky. They bite and sting, chew up gardens, and sometimes transmit dangerous diseases. Yet for all the problems some insects cause us, most are profoundly important to Earth's health—and to ours.

Insects pollinate most flowering plants—including at least fifty crops that humans depend on for food. Larger insects eat small and harmful insects that might otherwise infest our homes and farms. Many insects eat dead plants, while larvae sometimes feed on decomposing animals. In the process, these insects return nutrients to the soil, nourishing living plants that, in turn, feed so many other creatures.

CHAPTER TEN

ECHINODERMS

There's an interesting trend in the common names of the members of phylum Echinodermata: sea star, sea lily, sea cucumber, sea biscuit, sand dollar, sea urchin. See the trend? That's because this last group of invertebrates can only be found when you head out for a walk on the beach or put on your scuba gear and dive to the seafloor. Echinoderms can't live on land or in freshwater—they make their homes only in the salty oceans.

ON THE SURFACE

Echinoderm is Greek for "spiny-skinned," and that's a very accurate description. The external surfaces of these animals are covered in bumps, ridges, needles, and thorns. These pointy decorations are part of a body structure that only one other in vertebrate group, the cephalopods, has: an internal skeleton, or *endoskeleton*. Like the shells of mollusks, this endoskeleton is made of calcium carbonate, a chemical that creates a sturdy and lasting framework that survives even after the echinoderm dies.

Look at the endoskeleton through a microscope and you'll see calcium carbonate crystals that branch out and wind around each other to form solid plates. Neighboring plates interlock, like snapped-together pieces of a jigsaw puzzle. Sea stars have skeletons with loosely joined plates that create an intricate, lacy pattern. This structure makes the arms flexible and gives them the ability to lie flat, bend, or mold around rough surfaces. In sea urchins and sand dollars, the plates fit together so closely that it's hard to see them individually. Sea cucumbers have gone a different route—their plates are microscopic and don't form a solid skeleton at all.

Most echinoderms wear spiny weapons right on their backs, yet some have additional defenses. A long-spined sea urchin's venom is

101

Is it Odd to be Odd-Numbered?

While echinoderm larvae have bilateral (two-sided) symmetry, as adults they're radially symmetric (built around a central point, like jellies). The body of an adult echinoderm is almost always arranged in a pattern based on the number five. There can be five arms, or ten, or twenty-five. A few species have four or nine arms, or some other arrangement that's not divisible by five—though no one yet knows why. This five-part arrangement might seem odd, but it has a few benefits.

First, this shape means that sea stars and their relatives aren't limited to walking only forward and backward to escape danger or to search for food and mates.

Instead, sea stars can move in almost any direction.

Another advantage of the sea star's skeleton is its engineering. The arms are hinged together at a central disk, providing a solid frame that still allows each arm to move independently. It may have occurred to you that having six arms, or some other even number, would make sea stars nicely symmetric. That's true, but this even arrangement would also weaken the skeleton. The meeting of each opposite pair of arms would create "fracture zones" along which the animal could easily be split in half. No such seams are created when odd numbers of arms meet, so the skeleton is much stronger.

released when a spine breaks through an attacker's skin, causing searing pain. Most humans have nasty allergic reactions when they come in contact with the crown-of-thorns sea star. Their spines, 2.4 inches (6 centimeters) long and extremely sharp, are covered in skin that secretes several kinds of poisons. The beautiful, pink flower sea urchin has a different method of defense. Its back is covered in stalks, each of which is equipped with a set of venom-tipped pincers. The pincers can continue to bite and release toxins even after they're broken off. The pink flower urchin is the most venomous echinoderm, and under certain circumstances it can be lethal even to humans.

LOOKING DEEPER

There's no right or left side to an echinoderm, and you won't find a head or a tail. Instead, the echinoderm's body is organized around a central point. In some groups, all of the organs are contained within this space. In others, there are long arms that contain extensions of the organs.

Imagine the body of a sea star. On its top surface you'll find bumps and spines and, at the intersection of two of the arms, a small circle. This hole is the entrance to the *water vascular system*, which is found only among echinoderms. Water flows through the hole into the central disk, which houses a hollow ring canal from which radial canals branch off into each arm. These canals are lined with small bulbs, each of which has its own *tube foot* (like a cylindrical water balloon) that passes through the skeleton and skin, ending in a suction cup. Also on the star's top surface are eyespots, located at the tip of each arm, which allow the animal to sense light.

Now look at the bottom surface of the sea star. At its center is a mouth, sometimes equipped with teeth. Hundreds of tiny tube feet cover the arms. Oxygen is absorbed through the skin of the tube feet, which are also sensitive to touch and odors. Tube feet are also involved in food collection, and the animal uses them to walk and hold onto surfaces. The water vascular system works like a hydrostatic skeleton to move the tube feet. Water flows back and forth between a tube foot and its bulb (inside the arm). The tube foot gets a squirt of water when it needs to "flex" and extend, then returns the water to the bulb when relaxed.

Even if you've never been to the ocean, you're probably familiar with sea stars, common residents of shallow water near shorelines. Sea stars occur in nearly every color of the rainbow and sometimes are splotched with a variety of shades. Their common names hint at the diversity of "looks": candy cane star, pincushion star, bat star, crown-of-thorns star, and more. Sunflower stars have up to twenty-four golden, petal-like arms and bodies with a diameter of 2 feet (0.6 meters). The largest sea star species may reach over 3 feet from arm-tip to arm-tip, while the smallest is no more than three–quarters of an inch (1.9 centimeters) across.

They may be slow movers, but sea stars have no problem finding food. They usually eat bivalves. The star's challenge is opening its prey's locked–up shells. It does this by standing over the bivalve, attaching tube feet to either side of the shell, and pulling very hard. Once there's a little crack, the star pokes one of its two stomachs out through its mouth and inserts it between the bivalve's shells. Digestive enzymes go to work dissolving the meat, and the star sucks its food right up.

The second group of stars includes brittle stars and basket stars. The brittle star's five arms are long and snakelike. They're

The water vascular system of echinoderms controls the tube feet, which are used to walk, grip surfaces, gather food, and absorb oxygen.

beautiful to look at, but never touch a brittle star—its arms break right off, like dried twigs from a tree branch. Basket stars also have five arms, but appear to have many more. Each arm bears many curling branches that are waved in the water to capture floating food. Basket stars are common in some of the coldest waters in the world, including the Arctic Ocean.

BEYOND THE STARS

Sea cucumbers look nothing like sea stars. Oddly, their bodies are bilaterally symmetrical, soft, long, and tube-shaped like their namesake vegetables. But the five-part division of the body remains—there are five radial canals in their water vascular systems and five rows of tube feet. Around the sea cucumber's mouth are long, mucus–covered tube feet that function as tentacles for feeding. The animal uses its tentacles to sift the sand for food, particles of which stick to the mucus.

Sea urchins and sand dollars are round-bodied instead of star-shaped. Urchins look like spine-covered balls creeping along on the seafloor. The "ball" is called a *test*, a hollow endoskeleton that contains all the animal's organs. Spines vary in shape, size, and color: short, long, needlelike, or thick and round like pencils. They may be purple, red, orange, or even striped. A sea urchin's food of choice is seaweed. The tough blades are chewed up by the Aristotle's lantern, a toothy, tulip-shaped structure inside the urchin's mouth. The sand dollar looks even less like an animal than the urchin. Its body is flattened and its spines are short, resembling a beard covering the pancake-shaped test. Dried sand-dollar tests often wash up on beaches, especially after storms stir them up from the seabed. Look at the top surface and you'll see a pattern resembling the impression of a five-leafed plant, at the center of which there's a tiny, perfect star. Turn the test over and you'll find

Greedy, Greedy

Change is a common event in nature. Individual animals live and die, and species evolve and go extinct. Likewise, the number of individuals in a population often grows larger, then smaller, and then larger again. More often than not, these changes occur in response to two forces: the availability of food and the number of predators in the area.

When there's a population explosion among crown-of-thorns sea stars, coral reefs suffer. These outbreaks may be the result of human-caused water pollution, which causes algae to blossom. With all that food floating around, crown-of-thorns larvae (which are planktonic) have plenty to eat, so they are more likely to survive to adulthood. Stars may blanket a reef system and greedily eat up the living corals, leaving only coral skeletons behind. A second possible cause of crown-of-thorns outbreaks may be overhunting—when humans kill their predators, like triton mollusks and puffer fish, there is nothing to prevent an explosion of the star population.

Another greedy echinoderm is the purple sea urchin, a common resident of kelp beds along North America's Pacific Coast. Kelp fronds, up to 100 feet (30 meters) in length, form a kind of underwater forest that is home to a lively and diverse community of both invertebrate and vertebrate animals. Under normal circumstances, urchin populations are controlled by sea otters. Otters eat many varieties of invertebrates, but purple sea urchins are their favorite. In fact, the bones of sea otters often turn purple from the pigments in their urchin-food. When humans kill otters, urchin populations may expand quickly and eat the kelp. Urchins can destroy a kelp forest in a short time, leaving all its residents homeless and without food.

Sea urchins feed on blades of kelp, a variety of sea-weed. Without sea otters to control their populations, urchins can quickly wipe out an entire kelp bed.

a network of winding grooves that lead to the mouth. In the living animal, tube feet collect food particles and pass them into these grooves, which are filled with mucus. Food simply slides along the mucusy channels and into the mouth.

Of all the echinoderms, sea lilies and feather stars may be the loveliest. Their bodies are deceptively flowerlike. They're often elevated on tall stalks and may even attach themselves to surfaces with "roots." Feathery arms (in multiples of five) radiate like petals from a central disk. To feed, sea lilies spread their arms wide. Tube feet collect bits of floating food and pass them to the mouth on the upper surface of the central disk.

Scientists were surprised to discover a "new" group of echinoderms in 1986, which they named sea daisies. These round, flat, armless animals are less than half an inch (1 centimeter) in diameter and seem to prefer deep ocean habitats where they can feed on wood that has become waterlogged and has sunk to the seafloor.

MAKING THE CONNECTION

Scientists group organisms based not on when they evolved, but on the relationships between them. Shared physical characteristics and larval or embryonic (fertilized egg) stages are useful in determining these connections. Clades, or biological family trees, are drawn to show the links. These clades are works in process, constantly changing as researchers discover new fossils and look more closely at DNA. The order of chapters of this book reflects an invertebrate clade that many scientists agree on today.

Their appearance at the end of our list doesn't mean that echinoderms evolved last, however. Scientists have identified about 13,000 fossil species of echinoderms, and there are another 7,000 species living today. The most ancient echinoderm may be a creature from southern Australia, called *Arkarua adami*, whose five-part, 0.4-inch (10-millimeter) "footprints" are fossilized in rocks that are almost 600 million years old.

So what's the relationship that places echinoderms at the end of the invertebrate line? The answer is revealed when we compare the eggs and early life stages of echinoderms with those of lancelets and tunicates, the most primitive members of the phylum Chordata. As it turns out, the embryos of echinoderms, tunicates, and lancelets go through the same process of development. And although adults of these animals look radically different, their larvae are almost identical. Echinoderms and primitive chordates apparently shared a common ancestor and then split off in separate evolutionary directions about 500 million years ago.

Lancelets are tiny ocean-dwellers named for their knifelike shape. It's hard to tell a lancelet's head from its tail, but look closely and you'll find a fringe of tentacles surrounding its mouth. Lancelets often burrow into sand or mud and leave just these "arms" exposed, sweeping food and water into their mouths. When they do move, lancelets swim like fish. A flexible rod called a notochord runs like a thin wire down the lancelet's back for support. (This "chord" gives the phylum Chordata its name.) Just above it lies a nerve cord, which also stretches from head to tail.

Slit-shaped gills are used to filter food particles and oxygen from the water.

Adult tunicates, by contrast, look like transparent or brightly colored, balloonlike bags. A tunicate lives attached to the seafloor or some other hard, underwater surface and feeds by sucking water into its body through a tubelike siphon on its "head." Wastes are flushed out through another siphon on its belly. Tunicate larvae look quite unlike the adults, however. Instead, they resemble lancelets—their bodies contain a notochord, a nerve cord, a tail, and gill slits.

The third group of chordates, which probably evolved from tunicates, is the subphylum Vertebrata. You might know these animals as fish, amphibians, reptiles, birds, and mammals. Hard as it may be to guess by looking at them, sea stars, sea cucumbers, sand dollars, and other echinoderms are your closest invertebrate relatives.

A MUDDLE OF MINIATURE BEASTS

Most taxonomists divide animals into thirty-five phyla. The vertebrates and their ancestors make up one phylum, while all the others are invertebrates. Invertebrates are delightfully diverse and include 95 percent of the animal species currently living on Earth. While all these little animals might seem insignificant to us, they provide an important reminder: evolution doesn't always move toward large or complex forms of life. Indeed, many of the most amazing living things come in small packages.

G l o s s a r y

Animal — A multicellular, living thing that eats other living things

Appendage — An extension of the body, such as an arm, a leg, or an antenna

Asexual reproduction — Reproduction without the mixing of genes from two individuals

Atoms — The smallest particles of a chemical element that can exist independently

Bilateral symmetry — A body shape in which the right side is a mirror image of the left side

Binomial nomenclature — The system of giving two names to plants and animals, consisting of a generic name (genus) followed by a species name

Biodiversity — The total number of unique species on Earth at any given time

Bioluminescence — The ability to produce light through chemical reactions inside the body

Book lung — A sac-shaped organ found in arachnids and some other invertebrates, which contains page-like stacks of membranes used to absorb oxygen

Camouflage — A form of concealment that helps an animal blend into its environment

Carbon dioxide — A chemical common in air and water that is produced by animal respiration and used by plants in photosynthesis

Carnivore — A meat-eating animal

Cell — The basic unit of life that contains an organism's unique genetic information

Cephalothorax	A combined head and thorax common in chelicerates
Cerebral ganglion	A grouping of nerves in the head
Chelicerae	Fanglike feeding parts found on the heads of spiders and scorpions
Chitin	A nonliving chemical compound that forms the hard exoskeleton of arthropods
Chromosome	A "package" of DNA and protein found in the nucleus of every cell
Cilia	The tiny hairs on organisms that can produce a water current or aid in swimming
Circulatory system	A fluid-based system that transports oxygenated blood throughout an animal's body
Clade	A biological "family tree" that diagrams genetic and evolutionary relationships among organisms
Clitelum (plural clitella)	The swollen outer ring of annelids from which cocoons are formed
Clone	An offspring that is genetically identical single parent
Coelom	A fluid-filled internal body cavity that contains organs
Collar cells	Lightbulb-shaped cells that line the body cavities of sponges; they are involved in feeding and other body functions
Colony	A group of individuals of the same species living close together and dependent upon one another
Complete metamorphosis	The total change in body shape

experienced by the larvae of some insects to reach adulthood

Compound eyes Eyes with many lenses that are common in insects and horseshoe crabs

Crop A widened part of the digestive tract located just below the mouth of some insects that works to grind or store food before digestion

Cuticle Thick skin

Cyanobacteria Microscopic, single-celled, photosynthetic bacteria that were among the first living organisms on the planet and that are the most common organisms on the planet today

Decomposer An animal that feeds on dead plants and animals, breaking them down to basic nutrients and chemicals that are returned to the environment

DNA (deoxyribonucleic acid) A double-stranded protein that contains genes, which determine certain characteristics of an organism's appearance or behavior

Dormant In a state of suspended animation, like seeds

Endoskeleton A skeleton found under the skin

Epidermis The outer layer of cells covering the body of an animal

Evolution Change over time that adapts a species to its environment and, through the process of natural selection, produces new species

Exoskeleton A hard, external skeleton that covers an animal's soft body parts

Extinction The death of all individuals of a species

Flagella Whiplike hairs, longer and less numerous than cilia, used by animals for locomotion and creating water currents

Fossil The ancient remains, imprints, or trace of an organism that is preserved in rock or some other material

Gastrodermis The layer of cells lining the hollow body cavity of cnidarians

Gene A section along a DNA molecule inherited from an individual's parent that determines part of that individual's appearance or behavior

Genus A name shared by a group of very closely related organisms

Geologic time The long history of Earth, marking all the events that have shaped the planet and the living things that have evolved and gone extinct

Gill An organ that collects oxygen from water

Gizzard A muscular organ used by insects, crustaceans, and some worms to grind food into a pulp before digestion

Gravity The attraction between particles of matter and, in particular, between the mass of Earth and smaller particles

Habitat The place in which an organism lives

Herbivore An animal that eats plants

Hirudin A chemical in the saliva of leeches that thins the blood of a host upon which the leech feeds

Hydrostatic skeleton	A support system that is created by enclosing body fluids inside an "envelope" of skin
Incomplete metamorphosis	A process of change that occurs in some insects in which larvae look like small adults but undergo several molts before reaching maturity
Invertebrate	An animal without a backbone
Joint	The point(s) on an animal's limbs or antennae where movable parts meet
Larva (plural larvae)	An immature creature that looks different from its adult form
Lava	Molten rock that erupts or flows from within the Earth
Lungs	A pair of sac-shaped organs used in breathing, the tissues of which absorb oxygen into the bloodstream and pass carbon dioxide wastes out of the blood
Mantle	The fold of skin in mollusks that contains the internal organs
Mass extinction	The extinction of a large number of species over a relatively short period of time
Medusa (plural medusae)	The free swimming stage of the life cycle of cnidarians and ctenophores
Mesoglea	A jellylike substance found between the external and internal cell layers, particularly in cnidarians
Metamorphosis	A change from larval to adult form that is controlled by hormones
Molt	The process of shedding and replacing skin or a shell

Mutation	A change in the arrangement of genes that may occur during cell division, which may result in the expression of a new trait
Natural selection	The mechanism by which evolution occurs, in which the environment favors individuals best suited to survive and reproduce
Nematocyst	A kind of stinging cell found on the tentacles of cnidarians
Neoblasts	Special cells that can multiply and develop into any other kind of body cell; possibly involved in the invertebrate regeneration
Nucleotides	The basic molecular units that build nucleic acids, the parts of DNA
Nucleus (plural nuclei)	The part of a cell that controls cells functions and cell division and that builds proteins
Organelles	The specialized parts of a cell that perform functions similar to the organs of multi-cellular creatures
Ovipositor	An organ used by female insects to deposit their eggs
Ozone	A form of oxygen found in Earth's atmosphere that absorbs ultraviolet light from the Sun
Paleontologist	A scientist who studies Earth's geologic history by finding and observing the fossilized remains of ancient organisms
Palpus (plural palpi)	One of the paired segmented mouthparts found among many invertebrates, used in touch, feeding, and/or smell

Parapodia	Small appendages protruding from the sides of the body, especially in polychaetes
Parasite	An organism that obtains its nutrients from the bodies of other animals or plants
Parthenogenesis	A rare reproductive strategy in which an unfertilized egg develops into an adult animal
Pedipalps	Mouthparts found on arachnids that are used to grab and hold food
Pharynx	A thick, muscular part of the upper digestive tract in some invertebrates, used in sucking and swallowing
Photosynthesis	The chemical conversion of sunlight into energy
Plankton	A diverse group of tiny, often microscopic, plants and animals that float in bodies of water
Pigment	A substance found in the cells of organisms that provides color
Polyp	The attached, nonswimming stage of the life cycle of cnidarians
Proboscis	A tube-shaped extension of the mouth of some insects, used like a straw to suck in food
Radial symmetry	A body shape in which appendages are arranged around a central point
Radula	The rough, "toothed" tongue of mollusks, used to scrape food off surfaces
Regeneration	Regrowth of body parts, either after injury or during asexual reproduction
Scavenger	An animal who eats the remains of dead plants and/or animals

Segmentation	Division of the body into sections
Sexual reproduction	Production of offspring involving the exchange of DNA from two parents
Species	Any distinct group of organisms that can mate and produce fertile offspring in the wild (without human assistance)
Species name	The second name given to a species that is used to distinguish it from its closest relatives in the same genus
Spicules	Long, sharp, supportive structures found particularly in sponges and some mollusks
Spinnerets	The silk-producing organs of spiders
Spiracles	Openings on the body of arthropods through which air enters the body
Symbiosis	Close associations between individuals from species that usually benefit both
Systematics	The study of life on Earth in order to identify the evolutionary relationships between species
Taxonomy	A classification system used to name living things and group them based on their similarities
Tentacle	An arm-like organ used for touch and food-gathering
Test	A hard, hollow endoskeleton surrounding the bodies of some echinoderms, which encloses and protects all the organs
Thorax	The center of three body segments in arthropods
Tissues	Collection of cells that work together to conduct a particular body function and that

form organs in higher invertebrates
and vertebrates

Toxin   A chemical substance produced by an organism that acts as a poison

Tube feet   The small, flexible extensions that line the bottom surfaces of many echinoderms

Ultraviolet radiation   Light produced by the Sun at wavelengths just above visible light; in extreme doses, can cause mutations in organisms and high surface temperatures on the planet

Vertebrate   An animal with an internal bony skeleton and spinal column

Warning coloration   Bright skin colors advertising that an animal is either poisonous or mimicking the colors of a poisonous species

Water vascular system   A system of canals, bulbs, and tube feet that is controlled by the flow of water and is involved in movement, feeding, circulation, touch, and smell in echinoderms

FOR FURTHER READING

Bailey, Jim, ed. *The Way Nature Works.* New York: Macmillan Publishing Company, 1992.

Burnie, David. *How Nature Works.* Pleasantville, N.Y.: The Reader's Digest Association, 1991.

Cerullo, Mary M. *The Octopus: Phantom of the Sea.* Dutton, N.Y.: Cobblehill Books, 1997.

Conniff, Richard. *Spineless Wonders: Strange Tales from the Invertebrate World.* New York: Henry Holt and Company, 1996.

Fleisher, Paul. *Life Cycles of a Dozen Diverse Creatures.* Brookfield, Conn.: The Millbrook Press, 1996.

Gowell, Elizabeth Tayntor. *Life in the Deep Sea.* Danbury, Conn.: Franklin Watts, 1999.

Hubbell, Sue. *Waiting for Aphrodite.* Boston: Mariner Books, 1999.

Lauber, Patricia. *Earthworms: Underground Farmers.* New York: Henry Holt, 1994.

McGavin, George C. *Insects, Spiders, and Other Terrestrial Arthropods.* New York: Dorling Kindersley Publishing, 2000.

Silverstein, Alvin, Virginia Silverstein, and Robert Silverstein. *Invertebrates (The Kingdoms of Life).* New York: Twenty-First Century Books, 1996.

RELATED ORGANIZATIONS

Center for Marine Conservation
1725 DeSales Street, Suite 600
Washington, DC 20036
(202) 429–5609
http://www.cmc–ocean.org

National Wildlife Federation
8925 Leesburg Pike
Vienna, VA 22184–0002
(800) 822–9919
http://www.nwf.org

The Nature Conservancy
4245 North Fairfax Drive, Suite 100
Arlington, VA 22203–1606
(800) 628–6860
http://nature.org

Rainforest Action Network
221 Pine Street, Suite 500
San Francisco, CA 94104
(415) 398–4404
http://www.ran.org/ran

Reef Relief
P.O. Box 430
Key West, FL 33041
(305) 294–3100
http://www.reefrelief.org

Wildlife Conservation Society
2300 Southern Boulevard
Bronx, NY 10460
(718) 220–5111
http://www.wcs.org

The Xerces Society
4828 S.E. Hawthorne Boulevard
Portland, OR 97215
http://www.xerces.org

YMCA Earth Service Corps
National Resource Center
909 Fourth Avenue
Seattle, WA 98104
(800) 733–YESC
http://www.yesc.org

RELATED INTERNET SITES

Biology Class/The Internet Science Room, Frontier High School
http://pc65.frontier.osrhe.edu/hs/science/bworm.htm
This site provides a good review of all three groups of worms—flatworms, roundworms, and segmented worms—with visual aids and links to major scientific sites about worms.

The Cephalopod Page
http://is.dal.ca/~ceph/TCP/index.html#intro
This is an accurate, interesting, and educational page devoted to cephalopods.

Comb Jellies
http://www.microscopy-uk.org.uk/mag/artmay98/comb.html
Wim van Egmond's Micscape Magazine article provides great background information and gorgeous photographs of these tiny wonders.

Evolution on the Web for Biology Students
http://www.iup.edu/~rgendron/bi112–a.htmlx
Developed for college students studying evolution, this site is complex but is helpful for clarifying concepts and exploring evolution in greater detail.

Geologic Time, Online Edition
http://pubs.usgs.gov/gip/geotime/
This site offers a close-up look at geologic time from the United States Geologic Survey.

Glendale City College, Marine Biology Pages–Echinoderms
http://home.earthlink.net/~huskertomkat/echina.html
This site offers interesting, readable information on echinoderm biology and ecology, including terrific images. It also has links to pages on tide pools on and other invertebrate groups.

The Insect Page
http://www.insecta.com
This fabulous website from the Spencer Entomological Museum at the University of British Columbia is fun, easy to navigate, and visually appealing for visitors of all ages and levels of knowledge. It contains a great glossary of terms relevant to insects as well as a close-up look at each insect order. And don't miss the Bug of the Month!

Marine Flatworms of the World
http://www.rzuser.uni-heidelberg.de/~bu6
The information on this Danish site contains much more scientific detail than most students will need, but it's worth a visit to see the photographs of marine flatworms.

Ocean AdVENTure
http://library.thinkquest.org/18828/index.html
This is another ThinkQuest site that contains an exciting, hands-on look at hydrothermal vents and the creatures that survive there.

A Spongy Adventure
http://library.thinkquest.org/26502/level1/home.htm
This ThinkQuest site, built for kids, gives a thorough and interesting review of sponge biology and natural history.

University of California's Museum of Paleontology Web Lift
http://www.ucmp.berkeley.edu/phyla/phyla.html
This site leads to pages on all invertebrate groups—their biology, classification, and fossil history (check "parazoa" for sponges). This is an invaluable resource!

INDEX

ABOUT THE AUTHOR

Christine Petersen is a biologist and educator who has spent much of her career studying the behavior and ecology of bats. When she isn't in the classroom or doing research, Ms. Petersen enjoys talking about nature with visitors in her local parks and writing about her favorite wild animals and wild places. She is also the co-author of several books in Grolier's True Books series. Ms. Petersen makes her home on a lake near Minneapolis, Minnesota.